The 3-MINUTE SPELL BOOK
for BUSY NEW WITCHES

LILY NIGHTSHADE

Table of Contents

BABY WITCH, YOUR MAGIC AWAKES! . . 7

INTRODUCTION . . . 8

The Heart of Magic...10
How to Perform a Spell..13
The Moon as Your Guide..18
Tools of the Craft...19
The Language of Spells..22

CHAPTER 1: ENCHANTED LOVE & CONFIDENCE. . . 24

Overthinking Words — Clear-Tone Message Charm........
....25
Nerves Before Connection — Velvet Nerve Veil...........26
 Fear of Putting Yourself Out There — Brave-Heart Magnet..27
Unclear Relationships — True North Love Compass........
....28
Confidence Wobble — Self-Glimmer Glamour.............29
Comparing Yourself — Mirror of Enoughness...............30
Emotional Heat — Cool-Waters Balance Spell..............31
Letting Go of the Past — Gentle Unbinding Thread.......32
Learning to Trust Again — Soft-Shield Opener.............33
Calling In Aligned Love — Respect-First Magnet............
....34

CHAPTER 2: MAGNETIC MONEY & PROSPERITY . . . 35

Financial Panic | Calm Ledger Seal 36
Slow Money Flow | Honeyed Draw Spell 37
Opportunity Drought | Beacon Sigil 38
Performance Anxiety | Presence Polish Charm......................................39
Debt Overwhelm | Knot-

Table of Contents

by-Knot Untangle 40
Impulse Spending | Pause-Pocket Ward 41
Stalled Savings | Cushion Jar Momentum 42
Low Side-Gig Energy | Client-Call Lantern 43
Self-Doubt in Applications | Path Opener 44
Self-Worth in Money | Worth-Anchor Spell........... 45

CHAPTER 3: BRIGHT STUDIES & TRAVEL WARDS . .
46
Exam Panic: Focus Seal.. 47
Procrastination Spiral: Task Spark Starter 48
Brain Fog: Clear Head Sweep 49
Time Blindness: Study Block Beacon 50
Group Challenges: Harmony Weave..................... 51
Commute Unease: Street Shell Ward 52
Travel Safety: Safe Seat Charm 53
Lost Items or Luggage: Return Tag Spell 54
Unfamiliar Spaces: Fresh Sweep Claiming............... 55
Travel Anxiety: Sky Calm Press............................ 56

CHAPTER 4 SACRED FRIENDS & FAMILY 57
Roommate Tension - Flow Pact............................ 58
Friendship Drift - Thread-Stitch Repair 59
Unwanted Questions - Shield Fold......................... 60
Homesickness - Hearth-Spark Comfort 61
Loneliness New Places - Open-Door Charm 62
Gossip Swirl - Mirrorback Deflection 63
Boundary Guilt - Grace Seal........................... 64
Holiday Anxiety - Peace-Path Prep 65
Family Spats - Bridge Ease................... 66
Rebuilding Trust - Tower Stonework.......
67

Table of Contents

CHAPTER 5: GENTLE HEALTH & HEALING ... 68

Insomnia Loop: Pillow Drift 69
Nightmares: Star Ward 70
Sick-Day Blues: Soothe Charm 71
Anxiety Spike: Ground Anchor 72
Burnout: Restore Pause Ritual 73
Head Tension: Quiet-Crown Ease 74
Body Neutrality Wobble: Kind Mirror 75
Shallow Breathing: Triangle-Calm Pattern 76
Pain Overwhelm: Ease-Within Pocket Spell 77
Morning Slump: Momentum Brew 78

CHAPTER 6: EVERYDAY PROTECTION & BOUNDARIES. 79

Nosy Neighbors: Doorway Drift Ward 80
Leaky Energy: Bubble Perimeter 81
Energy Vampires: Thread Severance 82
Rumors: Mirror Return Spell 83
Bedroom Unease: Night-Watch Water Guard 84
Heavy Thresholds: Salt Sweep 85
Workplace Negativity: Desk Shield 86
Phone Overreach: DM Gatekeeper 87
Password Anxiety: Sentinel Charm 88
After-Conflict Residue: Peace Diffuser 89

CHAPTER 7: SERENE MENTAL CALM & FORGIVENESS 90

Intrusive Thoughts Quiet-Mind Aegis 91
Shame Spiral Compassion Cloak 92
Old Grudge Release Cut 93
No Closure Seal Within 94
Self-Blame Forgiveness Charm 95

Table of Contents

Catastrophizing Grounded-Now Anchor 96
Perfectionism Freeze Done-is-Good Spell 97
Boundary Guilt Kind-Guard Affirmation............ 98
Fear of Trusting Open-Heart Ward 99
Rest Guilt Permission Rite................................100

CHAPTER 8: FLOWING CYCLES & HARMONY. 101
Cramps - Warm-Wave Ease 102
Mood Swings - Balance Spell 103
Bloat & Body Heaviness - Light Comfort 104
Fatigue - Gentle Rally Charm 105
Irritability - Cool-Edge Calm 106
Sleep Trouble - Moon-Nest Rest 107
Low Desire - Ember Rekindle........................... 108
Cycle Awareness - Rhythm Reminder 109
Stigma Stress - Quiet-Pride Shield 110
Doctor Visit Nerves - Advocacy Voice Charm 111

CHAPTER 9: CLARITY & RHYTHM OF TIME... 112
Overwhelm: Sorting it Out Spell..........................113
Stuck Slump: Block-Buster Thaw 114
Time Blindness: Tuner Rite 115
Fear of Mistakes: Safe Starter..........................116
Decision Paralysis: Yes-Meter Discernment........117
Routine Won't Stick: Habit Hook 118
Too Many Goals: Power Cut 119
Starting Trouble: Two-Minute Spark 120
Creative Block: Muse Tap Knock........................121
    Weekly Reset: Recast Wheel........................122

YOUR POWER, YOUR PATH 123

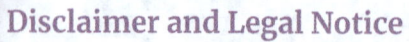

Disclaimer and Legal Notice

Baby Witch, your Magic Awakes!

Have you ever stared at your phone, heart racing, rewriting the same text a hundred times until your chest feels tight? Or walked into a room, wishing you could melt into the wall instead of feeling like every eye is on you? Or sat down to study, only to feel your brain slip into fog the moment you open your notes?

If you know those moments, this book is for you. Because magick is not about rare herbs or expensive tools. *It is not about joining a coven, calling on deities, or following a religion you do not believe in*. Magick is already in you, waiting for you to use it. And here, it only takes three minutes. I learned that the hard way…

I remember staring at a text thread until my stomach twisted. I typed, deleted, typed again, convinced I would ruin everything with the wrong words. Finally, I poured a glass of water, sprinkled in a pinch of salt, whispered the one line I truly wanted to send, and tapped it onto a sticky note. My chest loosened. I hit send without spiraling. That was the **Clear Tone Message Charm**, and it showed me that clarity does not come from overthinking. It comes from one true sentence.

Another time, before meeting someone new, my hands shook so badly I almost canceled. Instead, I slipped a bay leaf into my scarf and pictured it wrapping me in a quiet shield. When I walked into that coffee shop, the nerves were still there, but soft enough to let me breathe. That was the **Velvet Nerve Veil**, and it taught me that confidence is not about erasing fear. It is about carrying enough calm to let yourself shine.

And the night before a test, my brain was chaos. Ten tabs open. None of them my notes. I drew a circle on paper, set my pencil inside, and promised: inside this circle, I focus on one thing. I sipped water, pushed my phone away, and for the first time, the words stayed. That was the **Focus Seal**, and it reminded me that one small circle can protect your whole mind.

These are only three spells. Inside, you will find dozens more for love, friendship, money, travel, family, and beyond. Turn to the Table of Contents and see which ones call to you.

If you bought this book, it means you value yourself. If it was gifted to you, it means someone believes deeply in your spark. Either way, let this be your reminder: you are seen, you are valued, and you already carry the magick within you.

Take a breath. Turn the page.

Because the truth is simple. You are the spell.

Introduction

Welcome, kindred soul.

My name is Lily, and I have been walking the crooked, beautiful path of witchcraft for over a decade now. But my beginning was not a lightning strike or a grand revelation. It was quieter, softer, like the rustle of leaves in the wind. My journey did not start with spell books or movies, but with silence, grief, and a deep yearning for connection.

The First Spark

I was sixteen when I lost my grandmother. She was the heart of our family, gentle and wise, with a laugh that filled every corner of a room. After her passing, I felt hollow, drifting through days that all blurred together. One evening, I wandered into her garden, the place where she had spent countless hours coaxing life from the soil. I remember the way the air smelled that night: sweet earth, roses heavy with dew, and the faint smoke of a neighbor's fire curling up into the stars.

I sat by her rosemary bush and cried, whispering the things I wished I could tell her. And then something extraordinary happened. The wind rose suddenly, carrying the scent of rosemary straight to me, as though the plant itself had leaned down to listen. In that moment, I did not feel alone. I felt her, present, listening, comforting.

That night was my first true spell, though I did not have words for it yet. It was a conversation with the unseen, an act of reaching out and being answered.

Why I Turned to Witchcraft

From then on, I became fascinated with the small ways the world spoke to me. I noticed how candle flames flickered when I asked questions, how dreams grew vivid when I placed stones beneath my pillow, and how storms seemed to mirror my moods. Witchcraft was not about control. It was about listening, weaving myself into the rhythm of nature, and finding strength in unseen currents.

At first, I turned to magic to soothe my grief, but slowly it became more than that. It helped me reclaim joy, build courage, and carve out a life with meaning. I learned that spells are not just rituals. They are ways of aligning with the world around us, of saying yes to possibility.

Why I Wrote This Book

Over the years, I have met many people who feel called to magic but are unsure of where to begin. Some believe it must be complicated, or that it belongs only to those with years of study. Others fear they are not "witch enough" to start. I wrote this book to dissolve those fears.

This book is for the busy soul who wants to bring magic into daily life in small but powerful ways. Every spell here can be done in three minutes or less, because I believe magic should be simple, accessible, and woven into the fabric of your ordinary moments. You do not need elaborate tools or rare ingredients. What you need is intention, presence, and the willingness to believe in your own power.

I wrote this book because I know how transformative even the smallest ritual can be. It is my gift to anyone who has ever longed for connection, healing, or change.

What This Book Holds for You

This is not a book about complicated ingredients or elaborate ceremonies. It is about quick, powerful spells that you can weave into your everyday life, rituals you can perform in three minutes or less. Whether you are seeking protection, clarity, abundance, or simply a moment of peace, the magic here is accessible, practical, and deeply personal.

If you are reading these words, then the path has already opened for you. Maybe you are curious, maybe you are hurting, maybe you simply feel a tug toward something greater than yourself. Whatever brought you here, trust it. You found this book at exactly the right time.

Take a breath. Light a candle. Let us step together into the gentle, transformative world of spellcasting.

The Heart of Magic

There is so much more to magic than candles on an altar, jars of herbs, or poppets stitched with thread. Those are beautiful tools, yes, but they are not the source. Magic is alive in the world around us, in the whisper of the wind through trees, in the steady rhythm of ocean waves, in the way your heart quickens when you speak a wish aloud. Real witchcraft begins when you realize that you are already part of that living current, and always have been.

Before you light a single candle or tie a charm, the most important foundation of your practice is understanding what spellcasting truly is. It is not about waving a wand and bending the universe to your will. It is about aligning your energy with intention, focusing it, and sending it into the world like a ripple in a pond. The tools (herbs, crystals, incense, fire) are simply helpers, ways to strengthen your connection. But the true spark of power is already within you.

You are the only ingredient you will ever truly need.

When you step onto this path, you begin to uncover that hidden spark. With practice, it grows brighter, giving you the ability to heal, to shift, to create change in yourself and in the world around you. This is not about becoming someone else, but about remembering who you have always been: a person woven into the fabric of magic itself.

Why This Foundation Matters

To walk as a witch is to stand between worlds. You honor the past and those who walked this path before, while also shaping the present and opening doors to the future. Building a foundation rooted in history and awareness gives strength to every spell you cast. Without it, rituals can feel hollow, like a song with no melody.

That is why, before diving into charms and incantations, we will explore the who, what, and why of spellcasting. Together, we will clear away common misconceptions, untangle the difference between witchcraft and Wicca, and ground ourselves in the ethics that keep our craft strong. These core concepts are not restrictions but stepping stones, giving you a firm place to stand as you begin to weave change into your life.

Once you have these essentials, you will be ready to cast with confidence, to set your intentions clearly, and to step boldly into your own power.

What Spellcasting Really Is

Spellcasting is not a mysterious art locked away in dusty grimoires. It is simply focused intention, the act of taking a thought or desire and shaping it into something real. In truth, everyone casts spells, often without knowing it. When you whisper a wish before blowing out birthday candles, you are casting. When you carry a lucky charm into an exam, you are casting. When you picture yourself succeeding and feel your whole body align with that vision, you are casting.

To the outside world, these small rituals are invisible, even ordinary. But inside, they are powerful, because they are energy put to work.

The Nature of Energy

Magic is the current that flows through all things. It is not inherently good or evil. It is neutral, like fire, which can warm your home or burn it down. The morality of magic rests in the intention of the one who wields it.

We experience energy all the time. Have you ever felt someone step behind you before they touched you? A tingling, a sudden awareness? That was energy brushing against your own. Spells simply direct that same current with clarity and purpose.

Many mind-body practices are forms of casual energy manipulation. Yogis move energy through breath and posture. Reiki practitioners channel it through the palms of their hands. Monks raise and focus it through prayer, chant, and meditation. Acupuncturists guide it with needles, while tai chi practitioners shape it through movement. All of these practices are cousins to spellwork. They show us that energy is not abstract or imaginary. It is something that can be felt, directed, and used.

The Roots of Spellcasting

The word spell comes from the Anglo-Saxon spel, meaning "story" or "saying." Spells were once understood as words woven with power, stories spoken into being. Ancient Egyptians carved spells into tomb walls to guide souls to the afterlife. Norse cultures etched runes into wood and stone as protective charms. Folk healers across the world whispered incantations over herbs, waters, and flames.

History also shows us the shadows: centuries of persecution where witches were hunted for carrying this knowledge. From the Malleus Maleficarum in 1486 to the Salem trials in 1692, spellcasters were branded as dangerous. Yet despite fear and suppression, the craft endured. Witches carried it quietly in kitchens, gardens, and whispered blessings. In modern times, witchcraft has bloomed again, reminding us that the practice of shaping energy is as old and natural as storytelling itself.

Hedge Witches and Plant Allies

Among the many paths of witchcraft, hedge witches are known as "hedge riders," those who step between this world and the Otherworld. Their craft is liminal, rooted in thresholds, dreams, and spirit work.

They often practice herbalism, brewing potions, crafting salves, and tending to plants as allies.

Some hedge witches choose to cross the veil through altered states of consciousness. Historically, folk witches and shamans in Europe used entheogenic plants. Flying ointments, nightshades, mushrooms, and other fungi, to journey beyond the ordinary world. These substances were not toys or escapes, but sacred tools, dangerous if misused, powerful when respected. Today, some hedge witches continue this tradition, while many others prefer meditation, trance drumming, chanting, or lucid dreaming to reach the same connection.

The hedge witch's craft reminds us that magic is not only about ritual, but about relationship: with plants, with spirits, with the unseen world.

Different Witch Paths

Witchcraft is not one road, but a winding forest with many trails. Here are a few of the most common paths:

◊ Elemental Witch Works with earth, air, fire, and water. Green witches honor the earth with herbs and crystals. Sea witches turn to tides, shells, and storms. Hearth witches stir magic into their cooking and firelit homes.

◊ Secular Witch Works without deities, relying on symbols, intention, and personal power. Their craft is rooted in meaning, metaphor, and everyday ritual.

◊ Hedge Witch A traveler between worlds, skilled in herbalism, trance, and spirit work. Some use plant allies, including mushrooms, as gateways. Others rely on dreamwork and meditation.

◊ Eclectic Witch Gathers practices from many sources, creating a path that is fluid, personal, and evolving.

◊ Traditional Witch Walks older, structured paths tied to family, folk tradition, or ceremonial practices. These witches may inherit rituals passed down through generations.

Each path is valid, none more authentic than another. Witchcraft is not about fitting into a label, but about discovering what nourishes your soul.

Claiming Your Power

Spells are not quick fixes or shortcuts. They are not a way to control others or erase free will. They are invitations to align with possibility, to focus your energy on creating change. Like any art, they require patience, intention, and practice.

You already hold the spark within you. This book will help you recognize it, shape it, and let it grow brighter. No matter which path you choose, remember: magic is not something outside of you. It is already yours.

How to Perform a Spell

Crafting and Casting

Every spell has two halves: the crafting and the casting. Think of crafting as setting the stage and casting as the performance itself.

When I craft a spell, I begin by preparing the space. Sometimes that means wiping down my small wooden altar, sometimes it means walking barefoot in my garden and brushing fallen leaves away from a stump I like to use as an outdoor table. Clearing space is not just physical. It is energetic. I often clap my hands, burn a bit of incense, or simply imagine light sweeping through the area like a broom, pushing away anything heavy or unwanted.

Once the space feels ready, I create a circle of protection. This is less about walls and more about intention. Some witches call on deities or spirits. I often visualize a circle of soft golden fire rising around me, humming quietly, keeping out anything that does not belong. Once inside, I feel safe, grounded, and ready to raise energy.

Casting is where intention comes alive. It is the chant, the gesture, the candle lit, the cord tied. And when it is complete, I always close the circle with the same reverence I opened it, thanking the energy, letting it dissolve back into the earth, and sitting in stillness to observe what lingers.

Where to Cast Spells

Witches practice everywhere. Your spell space can be as grand as a dedicated altar room or as humble as a windowsill with a single candle. I have cast spells in my kitchen while stirring soup, in the bathroom with rose petals floating in the bath, and outdoors under a swollen full moon.

One of my first spells was cast in secret, in my childhood bedroom. I used a shoebox lid as an altar, a candle I borrowed from the kitchen, and a handful of wildflowers pressed between my schoolbooks. It was clumsy, uneven, but filled with heart, and it worked.

The truth is, the best place to cast is anywhere you feel safe and present. That could be your kitchen, a forest clearing, or the corner of a crowded apartment. What matters is your focus, not the grandeur of the space.

Creating an Altar

An altar is a witch's workbench, a sacred stage where magic takes form. It can be permanent or portable, extravagant or simple. Some witches follow tradition and face their altar north, adorning it with elemental tools: a bowl of salt for earth, incense for air, a candle for fire, a cup of water. Others fill theirs with crystals, feathers, shells, or objects that hold personal power.

I once built an altar on a beach, using driftwood as the base and seashells as offerings. The tide washed close as I cast my spell, and when the waves touched the altar, it felt as if the sea itself had answered me.

The point of an altar is not perfection. It is presence. Create one that reflects you and the spell you intend to cast. Let it change with the seasons, the moon, or your own moods.

Accessing Your Power

Magic begins with your own energy. Before you cast, you must learn to center, raise, and ground.

◇ Centering is finding your balance. Close your eyes, breathe deeply, and imagine your energy as a glowing sphere at your core. Feel it expand and contract with your breath.

◇ Raising energy is fueling your spell. You can build it by chanting, dancing, drumming, or simply focusing with fierce intent. Beginners sometimes drain themselves by using only their own energy. I learned this the hard way when I cast my first love spell as a teen and felt exhausted for days. Now, I draw from the world around me, the hum of a crystal, the pulse of the moon, the rhythm of the ocean. These energies combine with mine, strengthening my work.

◇ Grounding is releasing what remains. After casting, I kneel on the earth and press my palms to the soil, or if I am indoors, I imagine roots growing from my feet deep into the ground. On each exhale, I let the extra energy flow away, leaving me balanced again.

Solitary and Group Spellwork

Do you need a coven to cast spells? Absolutely not. Solitary spellcasting is deeply powerful. But some witches find energy magnifies in groups.

A coven is a structured community with shared rituals and often a priest or priestess leading the work. Some thrive in that environment, but others find it too rigid or prone to power struggles. I have been in circles that felt warm and supportive, and I have also walked away from ones that felt stifling.

A circle is looser, a gathering of witches who come together to celebrate the full moon, share spells, or simply sit in community. I love circles because they are fluid, open, and often filled with laughter.

Whether solitary or communal, the choice is yours. The only rule: never remain in a space where you feel unsafe or pressured.

Final Thoughts

Casting a spell is not complicated. It is a dance between your energy and the world. It is intention focused, shaped, and released. Whether at a grand altar or in the corner of your kitchen, your magic matters.

Start small. Whisper your wishes, light your candles, stir your soups with intention. With time, your craft will deepen, your energy will flow more easily, and you will find your own rhythm for crafting and casting.

Because in truth, every spell begins not with tools or circles, but with you.

Calendars, Seasons, and Sacred Tools

Opening

When I first began practicing witchcraft, I thought I could cast spells any time I wanted and get results. I lit candles when the mood struck. I whispered wishes into the air at random moments. Sometimes it worked, and sometimes nothing happened at all.

It took me years to understand why.

I was swimming against the current instead of with it. Magic, like everything else in nature, moves in cycles. The earth turns through seasons. The moon waxes and wanes. The sun marks solstices and equinoxes. When you align yourself with those cycles, your magic flows like water, carrying you instead of resisting you.

This is why calendars, seasons, and cycles matter. They are not rules. They are rhythms. And if you are just beginning, this is one of the most powerful lessons you can learn.

The Wheel of the Year

The Wheel of the Year is a cycle of eight festivals, called sabbats. Each sabbat marks a turning point in the seasons, and each one has its own flavor, its own energy, its own lesson.

Think of them as doorways. When you step through them, you step deeper into the rhythm of the natural world.

Samhain

October 31 in the northern hemisphere.

This is the witch's New Year, the last harvest, and the time when the veil between worlds is thin.

Why it matters: Samhain teaches us that endings are also beginnings. It is a time to honor ancestors, remember loved ones, and face the truth of cycles.

My first Samhain was quiet. I lit a single candle for my grandmother and placed her photograph beside it. I spoke to her as if she were still alive, and in the silence I felt her listening. That night changed me.

How you can start: Light a candle on Samhain night. Place a photo or object that reminds you of someone you love beside it. Speak their name. Thank them. That simple act is spellwork.

Yule

Winter solstice, the longest night of the year.

Yule is a promise. Even in darkness, light returns.

One year during a hard winter, I stayed up all night with only a candle. When dawn broke, I felt as if the sun itself whispered to me that I would get through it. And I did.

How you can start: On the longest night, write down one thing you are ready to release. Burn the paper safely. Then write one hope for the new year and keep it on your altar until spring.

Imbolc

February 1, the first stirrings of spring beneath the frost.

Imbolc is about clearing, quickening, and creativity.

I once cleaned my entire room on Imbolc. I opened windows, threw out old clothes, and dusted every shelf. When I lit a white candle afterward, the air felt lighter and so did I.

How you can start: Clean one corner of your space. Light a white candle. Speak a creative goal aloud. Treat it as if you are planting a seed.

Ostara

Spring equinox, when day and night are equal.

Ostara celebrates balance, renewal, and growth.

One year I planted herbs on Ostara. Each seed I pressed into the soil carried an intention. By midsummer, I was cooking with basil from my own spell plants.

How you can start: Plant something small, even in a pot. As you press it into the soil, whisper what you want to grow in your life.

Beltane

May 1, a fire festival of passion and beginnings.

Beltane celebrates love, creativity, and joy.

I once tied ribbons to a tree on Beltane. Each ribbon carried a wish. Whenever the wind moved them, I felt my desires flying into the world.

How you can start: Light a candle, dance in your kitchen, or wear something that makes you feel vibrant. Beltane is about celebrating your fire.

Litha

Summer solstice, the longest day.

Litha honors vitality, empowerment, and the sun at its peak.

On my first Litha, I lay in the grass all afternoon soaking in sunlight. That night I wrote a gratitude list and burned it in a candle flame. It felt like offering thanks directly to the sun.

How you can start: Spend time outside in the sun. Speak aloud one thing you are proud of this year.

Lughnasadh

August 1, the first harvest, also called Lammas.

Lughnasadh is about gratitude and preparing for colder days.

I baked bread for Lughnasadh once. Each knead was a spell of thanks. Sharing that bread with friends taught me that gratitude grows when you give it away.

How you can start: Bake bread or share food with someone. Speak your gratitude as you eat.

Mabon

Fall equinox, when day and night are equal once again.

Mabon is a festival of thanksgiving and balance.

I once cooked a simple meal with apples and squash for Mabon. A friend joined me, and we each named something we were grateful for. The room glowed with warmth.

How you can start: Cook a seasonal meal. Share it if you can. Speak gratitude before you eat.

The Moon as Your Guide

The sun marks the year, but the moon guides us each month. Her phases are a map for spellcasting.

◇ New Moon: The blank page. Begin projects or set intentions. Write a goal and place it under a candle.

◇ Waxing Moon: Energy builds. Perfect for growth, luck, or courage. Charge a charm each night under the waxing moon.

◇ Full Moon: Magic at its peak. Charge crystals, perform divination, or stand in moonlight and speak your desires.

◇ Waning Moon: Time to release. Write down what you want to let go of, burn it safely, scatter the ashes.

◇ Dark Moon: Rest and deep reflection. Journal, meditate, or sit in silence.

My first full moon spell was simple. I left a glass of water outside to soak up the moonlight. Drinking it the next morning felt like swallowing a piece of the night sky.

Tools of the Craft

Tools do not hold power on their own. They focus and amplify the power already inside you. Many of these tools have been used for centuries, but none are required to begin. Start with what you have, add slowly, and remember that intention is always the most important ingredient.

Book of Shadows

 Your magical diary, a place to record spells, dreams, rituals, and reflections. Witches throughout history kept grimoires or notebooks, often hidden for safety. A blank journal or even a simple folder on your computer can serve the same purpose.

Altar Bowl

 A vessel for offerings, herbs, salt, or water. Ancient cultures used bowls in ritual to hold sacred substances, from oils in Greece to incense in Egypt. Any small dish or bowl you already own can become an altar bowl once you dedicate it.

Mortar and Pestle

 A tool for grinding herbs, resins, or spices and infusing them with your energy. Healers and apothecaries relied on mortar and pestles for centuries. Beginners can use a kitchen set or even crush herbs with their fingers if that feels right.

Candles

 Flames are one of the most universal magical tools, symbolizing transformation and focus. Fire rituals have been used since humanity's earliest gatherings. White candles can stand in for any color, and even a tea light holds power.

Crystals

 Crystals are like batteries of energy that can store, amplify, and radiate intention. Egyptians, Chinese, and many ancient cultures used stones for healing and spiritual work. Beginners should start with clear quartz, cleansing it with water, salt, or moonlight between uses.

Incense

Sacred smoke clears space and creates ritual atmosphere. From temples in Egypt to churches and Buddhist monasteries, incense has always lifted prayers and purified the air. A single stick or even a bundle of dried herbs is enough to shift energy.

Divination Tools

Tarot cards, runes, pendulums, and mirrors help you listen to intuition and see patterns more clearly. Ancient oracles, Norse runestones, and scrying practices all share this purpose. Beginners can start by pulling one tarot card each morning or asking a pendulum simple yes or no questions.

Besom (Broom)

A broom sweeps away stagnant or negative energy and marks ritual space. In folklore, besoms symbolized both home and magic, often hidden near doorways for protection. A miniature broom on your altar or a small one dedicated only to ritual works well.

Poppets

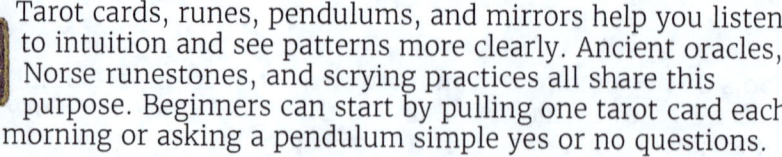

Handmade dolls used to represent people or intentions. Folk magic traditions across Europe and Africa used poppets made from cloth, clay, or wax for healing and protection. Beginners can stitch a simple felt doll and fill it with herbs connected to their goal.

Wand or Athame

The wand directs energy outward, while the athame, a ritual knife, channels energy symbolically. Both have roots in ceremonial and folk practices. A fallen branch or even your own finger can act as a wand until you feel ready for more.

My first wand was a willow branch I found after a storm. I smoothed it, tied a ribbon, and kept it close. It felt alive in my hand. That wand still rests on my altar today.

Chalice

A cup that represents water, emotions, and the womb of creation. Chalices have been part of sacred rituals across cultures, often filled with wine, water, or milk. Any cup dedicated to your practice can serve this role.

Pentacle

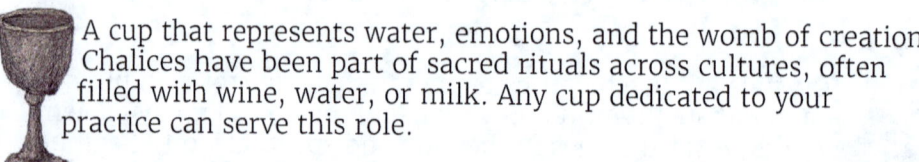

A flat disc marked with a five-pointed star inside a circle, representing the four elements and spirit in harmony. This symbol has roots as far back as Mesopotamia and medieval magic. Beginners can draw one on paper and place objects on it for charging or protection.

Feathers

Feathers carry the energy of air, communication, and spirit. Many cultures saw feathers as messages from the divine, from Egyptian crowns to Native American smudging tools. A feather you find outdoors can be cleansed and used to waft smoke or placed on your altar.

Anointing Oils

Oils infused with herbs and intention are used to bless, protect, and empower. Egyptians, Greeks, and early Christians used sacred oils in ritual and healing. Beginners can make their own with olive oil and kitchen herbs, using it to dress candles or anoint themselves.

Clothing and Adornment

What you wear when you practice matters more than beginners often realize. Clothing carries energy and mood. It shifts how you feel, and how you feel shapes your spell.

In some covens, witches wear robes. In some Wiccan traditions, witches work skyclad, which means without clothing, to feel closer to nature. I have done both. One time in a robe, I felt as if I were stepping into an ancient story. Another time beneath the stars, I felt free and powerful.

Most often, I wear something simple but meaningful. A soft dress I save for rituals. A necklace my grandmother gave me that now feels like a talisman.

How you can start: Pick one item to wear only when you practice. It can be a scarf, a crystal pendant, or even a simple shirt. Dedicate it by saying, "When I wear this, I step into my magic." Over time, that piece of clothing will carry your energy, and just putting it on will signal to your body that it is time for ritual.

Do not let all of this overwhelm you. You do not need to celebrate every sabbat, track every moon, or buy every tool. Start with one. Honor a single sabbat. Watch one moon cycle. Choose one tool. Dedicate one piece of clothing.

Each step roots you deeper into the rhythm of the world. That is why these details matter. They connect your magic to something greater, to the pulse of earth and sky.

And when you begin to move with those rhythms, you will feel it. Your spells will grow stronger, your practice more natural, and your heart more connected.

That is where your real power begins.

The Language of Spells

When I first started spellwork, I stumbled over the basics. Books tossed around words like cleanse and anoint as if I was supposed to know exactly what to do. I didn't, and maybe you don't either. So let me walk you through the most common instructions you will see in this book, the simple foundations that make every spell stronger.

Clear the Air

Before any spell, I cleanse my space. I sweep away both dust and the invisible heaviness that lingers in rooms. Witches have done this for centuries with smoke, salt, or sound, because energy clings the way cobwebs do. For you, it might be incense, clapping your hands in the corners, or simply saying, "This space is clear, this space is mine." The moment you feel lighter, the magic has already begun.

Wipe the Slate Clean

Tools and ingredients come with baggage. Every hand that touched them left a trace. That is why purification matters. A crystal at a market stall, a candle from the store shelf, even a spoon from your kitchen all deserve a reset. Pass it through smoke, rinse it in saltwater, or hold it and imagine light pouring through it. You will feel the shift when it is ready.

Moon-Soaked Water

Water holds memory, which is why so many cultures treated it as sacred. When I first left a jar of water under a full moon, I swore it looked brighter the next morning, as if it had drunk the light. You can make moon water by leaving a bowl or jar out overnight during the full moon, then using it to anoint, bless, or sip during rituals. If the sky is cloudy, it still works. The moon always finds a way in.

Stone Recharge

Crystals are like little batteries. They hum with energy when full, and grow dull when overworked. The simplest recharge is to place them under the full moon, though sunlight and earth work too if the stone allows. If you are in a hurry, hold it in your palm, breathe deeply, and see it glowing again. You will know it worked when the stone feels alive in your hand.

Breathing Life Back In

Spells do not last forever. A jar, charm, or pendant will fade the same way perfume does. When that happens, I repeat part of the original spell. Maybe I smoke it again, anoint it with oil, or speak the same words. The object drinks it up like water, and suddenly it feels potent again. Regular recharging keeps your magic fresh.

Oils of Power

To anoint is to bless with oil, and it is one of my favorite little rituals. The act itself is ancient. Priests, queens, and healers all used oil to make the ordinary sacred. For you, it can be as simple as dipping a finger in olive oil and drawing a symbol on a candle or your own skin. A few drops are all it takes to seal an intention.

Through the Looking Glass

Scrying sounds mysterious, but really it is the art of gazing. Our ancestors did it in fire, in water, and in smoke. I like to stare into a candle flame until my mind quiets and images begin to drift forward. You may see shapes, colors, or nothing at all at first. The key is trust. Your intuition is speaking even if it whispers.

Wand in Hand

A wand is not for sparks or lightning bolts. It is for focus. I think of mine as an extra finger that points energy where I want it to go. When I trace a circle in the air, I imagine a barrier of light forming. When I point at a crystal, I imagine energy flowing into it. A stick from the park works just as well as a carved wand if you treat it as sacred.

Breath Into Stone

Imbuing is simply filling an item with your energy. I remember the first time I tried it. I held a pebble in my hand, whispered a wish, and felt it warm up. That warmth was my intention sinking in. To do it, hold your item, breathe slowly, and picture your desire glowing inside it. That glow is what makes it more than just an object.

Why These Steps Matter

These instructions are not filler, they are the bones of spellwork. Cleansing makes room, purification wipes history, charging fills with power, and imbuing seals the deal. Scrying and wands sharpen your focus, while oils and recharging keep your tools alive. If you practice these often, they will become as natural as brewing tea, and that is when the magic truly clicks.

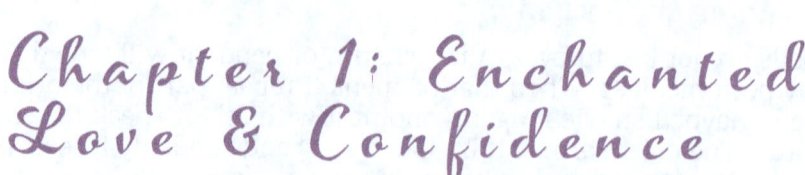

Chapter 1: Enchanted Love & Confidence

"Choose the love that begins with you."

The night I learned the Clear Tone Message Charm, my phone screen felt like a cliff. It was 1 a.m. My mug had a crack shaped like a tiny river. I kept rewriting the same text and deleting it. I finally lit a tea light, breathed in for four, out for six, and whispered the words into the steam. I pressed send while my thumb shook. The reply came a minute later. Not perfect. Real. I felt my ribs loosen like a tight belt. Next day, I used Velvet Nerve Veil before a first date. I pressed my scarf to my face, counted my breaths, and pictured a soft blue curtain around my chest. I walked in without that panicky buzz that makes you talk too fast.

One history example. In the Greek Magical Papyri, people wrote vowel strings to steady the voice and make speech clear. That told me our fear of speaking is old and normal, and that breath plus simple sound can change how we show up.

This chapter matters because love needs clarity and courage at the same time. These small rites help you say what you mean and hear what the other person truly says. If you are ready to show up as yourself and be met there, let's get started.

Overthinking Words — Clear-Tone Message Charm

I used to rewrite my texts until my thumbs hurt. Same with emails, same with deciding what to say in group chats. One night, I lit a candle, stirred honey and salt into water, and spoke the words: "Clear words, true voice." I sipped and felt my chest ease. The message I sent after flowed without effort, and for once, I didn't worry how it would land.

WHEN TO PERFORM

Before sending a message, posting online, or having a difficult conversation

TIME TO ALOT

5 minutes

WHERE TO PERFORM

Desk or bedside

INGREDIENTS/TOOLS

◊ Glass of water

◊ 1 pinch of salt

◊ 1 teaspoon honey

◊ White candle

◊ Spoon

Optional: Add rosemary for sharper clarity.

DIRECTIONS

1. Light the candle. Stir salt and honey into water.
2. Whisper: *"Clear words, true voice, flow with ease."*
3. Sip three times, picturing your throat glowing with calm light.
4. Speak, type, or send what you need without second-guessing.

Nerves Before Connection — Velvet Nerve Veil

I used to get shaky before first dates, job interviews, even group hangouts. One night, I brewed chamomile tea, sweetened it with sugar, and whispered over the rising steam. As I sipped, I felt a calmness wrap around me like velvet. I walked into the room steady and warm instead of jittery.

WHEN TO PERFORM

Before meeting new people or stepping into an important moment

TIME TO ALOT

3 minutes

WHERE TO PERFORM

Kitchen

INGREDIENTS/TOOLS

- ◊ Chamomile tea bag
- ◊ 1 teaspoon sugar
- ◊ Small piece of lemon peel
- ◊ Mug
- ◊ Hot water

Optional: Add a drop of vanilla extract for gentle charm.

DIRECTIONS

1. Brew tea, add sugar and lemon peel.
2. Hold the cup in both hands and whisper: *"Calm and charm, steady and warm."*
3. Sip slowly, imagining yourself surrounded by a velvet veil of confidence.

Fear of Putting Yourself Out There — Brave-Heart Magnet

I used to avoid confessing feelings, applying for jobs, or even posting creative work because I was terrified of rejection. One morning, I made toast sprinkled with cinnamon, spoke my courage into it, and ate it with steady breaths. That day, I submitted my application without fear.

WHEN TO PERFORM

Before asking for love, opportunity, or visibility

TIME TO ALOT

3 minutes

WHERE TO PERFORM

Kitchen

INGREDIENTS/TOOLS

◇ Slice of bread

◇ Butter or olive oil

◇ Sprinkle of cinnamon

◇ Glass of water

◇ Red cloth or napkin

Optional: Add honey for sweetness in the outcome.

DIRECTIONS

1. Spread butter, sprinkle cinnamon in a heart shape.

2. Place bread on red cloth and say: *"I magnetize love, brave and true."*

3. Eat, sip the water, and feel courage building in your chest.

Unclear Relationships — True North Love Compass

Sometimes it's a situationship. Sometimes a friendship that feels lopsided. Sometimes just not knowing what role you play in someone's life. I once stirred salt into water, lit a candle, and asked for guidance. The next morning, my gut knew the answer before my brain did.

WHEN TO PERFORM

When you're confused about where a relationship stands

TIME TO ALOT

4 minutes

WHERE TO PERFORM

Quiet table

INGREDIENTS/TOOLS

◊ Glass of water

◊ 1 pinch of salt

◊ Bay leaf (or laurel seasoning)

◊ White candle

◊ Pen and paper

Optional: Add cinnamon for clearer insight.

DIRECTIONS

1. Light the candle. Drop salt into water.

2. Hold bay leaf over the glass and whisper: *"Show me true north."*

3. Place the leaf under the candle, then free-write whatever thoughts come.

4. Trust the first feeling — that's your compass.

Confidence Wobble — Self-Glimmer Glamour

On certain mornings, I'd catch my reflection and sigh. But then I learned this little glamour: a dab of sugar water on my wrists, plus an affirmation. I felt myself sparkle from the inside, even if no one else noticed yet.

WHEN TO PERFORM

Before school, work, or social events when you feel "meh" about yourself

TIME TO ALOT

3 minutes

WHERE TO PERFORM

Bathroom or mirror

INGREDIENTS/TOOLS

- ◊ Small bowl of water
- ◊ 1 teaspoon sugar
- ◊ Mirror
- ◊ Cotton ball or tissue
- ◊ Pink candle (optional)

Optional: Add rose petals for extra love energy.

DIRECTIONS

1. Dissolve sugar in water.
2. Dip tissue and dab on wrists or behind ears.
3. Look in the mirror and say: *"I shine, I glow, I already know."*
4. Step out carrying that glimmer.

Comparing Yourself — Mirror of Enoughness

I used to scroll social media until I felt smaller than everyone else. One night, I wrote my name on a sticky note, placed it on my mirror, and traced it with honey water. It was a quiet, powerful reminder: I was already enough.

WHEN TO PERFORM

After comparing yourself to others

TIME TO ALOT

6 minutes

WHERE TO PERFORM

In front of a mirror

INGREDIENTS/TOOLS

- ◊ Small bowl of water
- ◊ 1 teaspoon honey
- ◊ Sticky note
- ◊ Pen
- ◊ Mirror

Optional: Add lavender for calming self-acceptance.

DIRECTIONS

1. Write your name on the note, place it on the mirror.
2. Mix honey with water, trace your name with your fingertip.
3. Say: *"I am already enough."*
4. Smile until it sinks into your reflection.

Emotional Heat — Cool-Waters Balance Spell

Sometimes jealousy, envy, or irritation rises like fire. I once filled a bowl with cool salted water, dipped my hands, and whispered balance. The heat eased. I was steady again.

WHEN TO PERFORM

When emotions flare hotter than you want

TIME TO ALOT

3 minutes

WHERE TO PERFORM

Bathroom or kitchen sink

INGREDIENTS/TOOLS

◊ Bowl of cool water

◊ 1 teaspoon salt

◊ Blue towel or cloth

◊ Your hands

Optional: Add cucumber slices for extra cooling.

DIRECTIONS

1. Dissolve salt in cool water.
2. Submerge your hands, breathe slowly.
3. Say: *"Cool waters wash, balance restore."*
4. Dry hands with the blue cloth, feeling calmer.

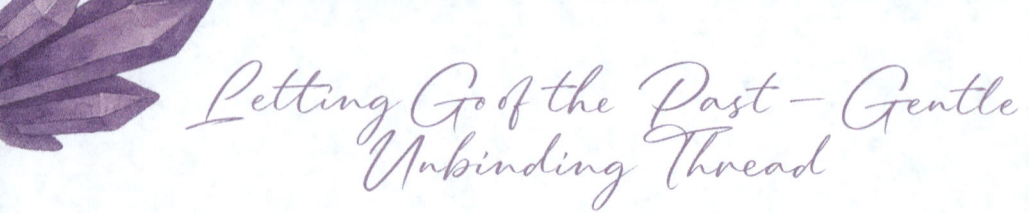

Letting Go of the Past — Gentle Unbinding Thread

I once tied a thread around my wrist, whispered a release, and cut it. It was the first time my chest felt lighter about an old breakup. This spell works for memories of friends, crushes, or even old versions of yourself.

WHEN TO PERFORM

When you're ready to release what's no longer serving you

TIME TO ALOT

4 minutes

WHERE TO PERFORM

Bedroom or quiet corner

INGREDIENTS/TOOLS

- ◊ Piece of string or thread
- ◊ Scissors
- ◊ Candle
- ◊ Glass of water
- ◊ Scrap of paper

Optional: Add incense or sage for cleansing.

DIRECTIONS

1. Tie the thread loosely around your wrist.
2. Say: *"The past is done, I choose the sun."*
3. Cut the thread, drop it in water.
4. Burn or discard the paper with their name or symbol.

Learning to Trust Again — Soft-Shield Opener

After betrayal, I locked my heart so tight no love could enter. This ritual softened the shield without tearing it down. I felt safe but not closed anymore.

WHEN TO PERFORM

When rebuilding trust in relationships or friendships

TIME TO ALOT

3 minutes

WHERE TO PERFORM

Anywhere quiet

INGREDIENTS/TOOLS

◇ White candle

◇ Pinch of sugar

◇ Pinch of salt

◇ Small bowl of water

◇ Spoon

Optional: Add rosewater for gentle openness.

DIRECTIONS

1. Light the candle. Stir sugar and salt into water.

2. Hold the bowl to your heart, whisper: *"Shield soft, heart open, safe to love."*

3. Dip fingers into water and touch your chest.

4. Picture a pink glow radiating around you.

Calling In Aligned Love — Respect-First Magnet

I once listed the kind of love I wanted… not just romance, but friendships, mentors, community. I placed the list under a glass of sugared water and lit a candle. Within weeks, I met people who matched the energy.

WHEN TO PERFORM

When you're ready to attract love, respect, or supportive people

TIME TO ALOT

3 minutes

WHERE TO PERFORM

Bedroom altar or bedside

INGREDIENTS/TOOLS

◊ Glass of water

◊ 1 teaspoon sugar

◊ Small piece of paper

◊ Pen

◊ Candle

Optional: Add rose petals for romance.

DIRECTIONS

1. Write down qualities of love or relationships you want.
2. Place glass of sugar water on top.
3. Light candle, say: *"Respect first, love aligned."*
4. Leave overnight, then keep the paper under your pillow.

Chapter 2: Magnetic Money & Prosperity

"Small wins compound."

I hit bottom on a kitchen floor with grocery receipts stuck to my socks. My head was loud. I drew a small square on the first page of my notebook and pressed my palm over it. Calm Ledger Seal is simple. Four slow breaths. Write the real numbers. No hiding. My pulse slowed enough for a plan. Later, I made a tiny Beacon Sigil on an index card and tucked it under my laptop. That week I wrote three honest emails about work I could do. One turned into a paying project. I did not win a lottery. I got steady enough to see and follow the next step.

One history example. In old Rome, shopkeepers carved Fortuna on doorways for luck in trade. It was a daily reminder to open the door, greet people, and keep accounts in order.

This chapter matters because money is not magic points. It is choices, timing, and relationships. Panic makes bad math. Calm makes paths you can walk. If you want your effort to turn into options you can keep, let's get started.

Quick question:

Are you finding this book helpful? Would you leave a quick review?

Even one sentence makes a huge difference and takes just a minute.

As a small author, your feedback not only lifts my heart. It also helps others find the support and hope they need.

Thank you for being part of this journey!

Financial Panic/Calm Ledger Seal

I made this on a night my bank app looked like a horror movie. My heart raced, so I kept it simple. Salt. Flame. Breath. I drew a small circle of safety on a plate and felt my chest loosen. It did not erase the bill, but it gave me a calm mind to solve it.

WHEN TO PERFORM THIS SPELL:

Saturday, or during a new moon

TIME TO ALLOT FOR THE SPELL:

10 minutes

WHERE TO PERFORM THIS SPELL:

Kitchen table or counter

INGREDIENTS/TOOLS:

◊ Small plate

◊ Table salt

◊ Bay leaf

◊ Pen

◊ Tea light candle

Optional: Add a drop of vanilla. Not required, but it adds a comforting, steadying vibe.

Directions

1. Wipe your surface. Place the plate down and breathe slowly.

2. Pour salt in a small circle on the plate. This is your calm zone.

3. Write your goal on the bay leaf, like "Rent paid" or "I stay steady."

4. Set the bay leaf inside the salt circle. Place the candle next to it on the plate.

5. Light the candle and say, "Mind like water, numbers align. From fear to focus, peace is mine."

6. Sit quietly for a few breaths. When the candle is done, tuck the bay leaf near your budget notebook or phone case.

Slow Money Flow / Honeyed Draw Spell

Tips were crawling, not rushing. I wanted a gentle nudge, not a storm. I stirred honey, cinnamon, and green tea into a sweet little magnet jar. The next day felt brighter, and the slow trickle turned into a steady pour.

WHEN TO PERFORM THIS SPELL:

Thursday or during a waxing moon

TIME TO ALLOT FOR THE SPELL:

12 minutes

WHERE TO PERFORM THIS SPELL:

Kitchen

INGREDIENTS/TOOLS:

- ◇ Small jar with lid
- ◇ Honey
- ◇ Ground cinnamon
- ◇ Green tea bag
- ◇ Tea light candle

Optional: Add a pinch of nutmeg for warmth and luck.

Directions

1. Clean your space. Set the jar in front of you.
2. Add one teaspoon honey to the jar. Sprinkle a pinch of cinnamon.
3. Steep the tea bag in a little hot water for one minute. Add one spoonful of the tea to the jar.
4. Close the lid and swirl clockwise three times while saying, "Sweet flow, steady and true, draw good money as I do."
5. Set the tea light beside the jar and light it. Watch the flame for one minute.
6. Keep the jar near your workspace or cash box. Swirl it once each morning.

Opportunity Drought / Beacon Sigil

The job boards felt empty, like calling into a canyon. I decided to light a beacon. Citrus, water, and a simple sign. That week, two leads pinged my inbox. Not magic like a movie, more like a lighthouse finally switched on.

WHEN TO PERFORM THIS SPELL:

Sunday morning or any sunrise

TIME TO ALLOT FOR THE SPELL:

9 minutes

WHERE TO PERFORM THIS SPELL:

Kitchen window or table

INGREDIENTS/TOOLS:

◊ Orange

◊ Bay leaf

◊ Marker

◊ Clear glass cup

◊ Tea light candle

Optional: Add a pinch of sugar to the water for "sweet" chances.

Directions

1. Wipe your space. Fill the glass with fresh water.

2. Draw a simple sigil or symbol for "open doors" on the bay leaf. Keep it bold.

3. Float the bay leaf in the glass. Peel a small strip of orange zest and drop it in.

4. Place the candle beside the glass and light it. Say, "Light to signal, paths reveal. Right doors open. This is real."

5. Let the candle burn safely while you polish a resume or send one message.

6. Later, pour the water at the base of a plant or outside. Keep the bay leaf in your wallet for one week.

Performance Anxiety/Presence Polish Charm

Before a big interview, my stomach fluttered like caged birds. I made a tiny polish with kitchen herbs, rubbed it on my pulse points, and suddenly I could hear my own voice again, clear and steady.

WHEN TO PERFORM THIS SPELL:

Morning of the event or Wednesday

TIME TO ALLOT FOR THE SPELL:

3 minutes

WHERE TO PERFORM THIS SPELL:

Kitchen sink or counter

INGREDIENTS/TOOLS:

◊ Lemon

◊ Rosemary (fresh or dried)

◊ Granulated sugar

◊ Olive oil

◊ Small bowl

Optional: Add a pinch of peppermint tea for sharp focus.

Directions

1. In the bowl, mix 1 teaspoon olive oil with a tiny squeeze of lemon.

2. Crush a pinch of rosemary and a pinch of sugar between fingers. Stir into the oil.

3. Rub a little on wrists and throat. Breathe in the scent.

4. Say, "Steady breath, grounded tone. I shine bright in my own zone."

5. Rinse hands, leave a thin scent on skin. Smile in the mirror.

6. Go speak like you already belong there.

Debt Overwhelm / Knot-by-Knot Untangle

I used to stare at a huge number and freeze. This ritual taught me to split the mountain into steps. Each knot became one action I could do today, not someday.

WHEN TO PERFORM THIS SPELL:

Saturday evening

TIME TO ALLOT FOR THE SPELL:

7 minutes

WHERE TO PERFORM THIS SPELL:

Kitchen table

INGREDIENTS/TOOLS:

- ◊ Kitchen twine
- ◊ Paper
- ◊ Pen
- ◊ Bowl
- ◊ Table salt

Optional: Add a black tea bag to the bowl for extra grit and focus.

Directions

1. Pour warm water into the bowl. Add a pinch of salt for strength.
2. On the paper, write the big worry at the top. Under it, list 3 small steps.
3. Cut a strand of twine. Tie one gentle knot for each small step.
4. Hold the twine over the bowl and say, "Big weight, break apart. Step by step, brave heart."
5. Dip the knotted part into the water, sealing your promise to act.
6. Tape the twine above your desk. Untie one knot each time you complete a step.

Impulse Spending / Pause-Pocket Ward

I kept grabbing snacks and cute extras. My wallet felt like a leaky bucket. This little charm became a gentle stop sign in my pocket. I reached for cash and felt the ward, then chose with care.

WHEN TO PERFORM THIS SPELL:

Wednesday, or before a shopping trip

TIME TO ALLOT FOR THE SPELL:

6 minutes

WHERE TO PERFORM THIS SPELL:

Kitchen counter

INGREDIENTS/TOOLS:

- ◊ Small zip bag
- ◊ White rice
- ◊ Bay leaf
- ◊ Black pepper
- ◊ Rubber band

Optional: Add one clove for protection.

Directions

1. Pour two spoonfuls of rice into the zip bag.
2. Sprinkle a tiny pinch of black pepper for boundaries.
3. On the bay leaf, write "Pause" on one side and "Plan" on the other.
4. Slip the leaf into the bag. Seal and wrap the rubber band around it once.
5. Hold it and say, "I choose with care, I keep my pace. My money rests in a safe place."
6. Keep it in your pocket or wallet. Touch it before any purchase.

Stalled Savings / Cushion Jar Momentum

I wanted a safety net and kept forgetting to start. This jar turned saving into a mini habit. The soft shake each morning felt like cheering for Future Me.

WHEN TO PERFORM THIS SPELL:

New moon or payday evening

TIME TO ALLOT FOR THE SPELL:

8 minutes

WHERE TO PERFORM THIS SPELL:

Kitchen shelf

INGREDIENTS/TOOLS:

◊ Clean jar with lid

◊ White rice

◊ Sugar

◊ Paper

◊ Pen

Optional: Tie a green ribbon around the jar neck for growth.

Directions

1. On the paper, write a clear goal like "First 100 saved."
2. Place the paper under the empty jar.
3. Add a thin layer of rice, then a sprinkle of sugar. Repeat once. Think cushion and sweetness.
4. Close the lid and say, "Grain by grain, sweet and sure. My savings grow, safe and secure."
5. Shake gently three times each morning. Add a pinch of rice or one dollar whenever you can.
6. When you hit the goal, replace the paper with a new goal and keep going.

Low Side-Gig Energy/Client-Call Lantern

After a long day, my side hustle felt dull. I needed spark, not exhaustion. Coffee, citrus, and flame turned into a tiny lighthouse for clients and courage.

WHEN TO PERFORM THIS SPELL:

Thursday afternoon or Monday morning

TIME TO ALLOT FOR THE SPELL:

9 minutes

WHERE TO PERFORM THIS SPELL:

Kitchen table

INGREDIENTS/TOOLS:

- ◇ Coffee grounds
- ◇ Orange peel
- ◇ Small plate
- ◇ Tea light candle
- ◇ Table salt

Optional: Add a pinch of ginger for bold action.

Directions

1. On the plate, trace a small circle of salt.
2. Inside the circle, make a ring with coffee grounds.
3. Cut the orange peel into a small star or heart and place it in the center.
4. Set the candle in the middle and light it. Say, "Bright and brave, I'm seen and heard. Right clients find me, spread the word."
5. While it burns, send one message, post one listing, or make one call.
6. When done, compost the peel and grounds. Rinse the plate. Repeat when energy dips.

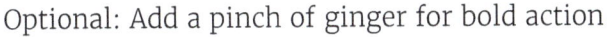

Self-Doubt in Applications / Path Opener

I kept telling myself the door would slam shut. Instead of quitting, I brewed a small path opener and felt my shoulders drop. I pressed submit with a steady hand.

WHEN TO PERFORM THIS SPELL:

First of the month or Sunday sunrise

TIME TO ALLOT FOR THE SPELL:

3 minutes

WHERE TO PERFORM THIS SPELL:

Kitchen window

INGREDIENTS/TOOLS:

- ◊ Fresh basil
- ◊ Lemon
- ◊ Bay leaf
- ◊ Glass cup
- ◊ Pen

Optional: Add one star anise for clear direction.

Directions

1. Fill the glass with water.
2. Write your name and one word on the bay leaf, like "Yes" or "Open."
3. Add a basil leaf and one thin lemon slice to the water. Float the bay leaf on top.
4. Hold the glass to the light and say, "Roads ahead, clear and wide. Worthy steps, I walk with pride."
5. Set it by the window while you finish one application task.
6. Pour the water into soil outside. Keep the bay leaf in your bag until you hear back.

Self-Worth in Money/Worth-Anchor Spell

I used to shrink my prices and say sorry for existing. This tiny anchor reminded me that my time is not a clearance rack. I carried it, and my voice stopped wobbling.

WHEN TO PERFORM THIS SPELL:

Friday or on a day you set prices

TIME TO ALLOT FOR THE SPELL:

3 minutes

WHERE TO PERFORM THIS SPELL:

Kitchen counter

INGREDIENTS/TOOLS:

- ◊ Bay leaf
- ◊ Olive oil
- ◊ Ground cinnamon
- ◊ Aluminum foil
- ◊ Tea light candle

Optional: Add a pinch of cocoa for richness and confidence.

Directions

1. Rub a drop of olive oil on the bay leaf. Dust a tiny pinch of cinnamon over it.
2. Hold it over your heart and say, "My work has weight. My voice is clear. I charge fair value. I honor my year."
3. Place the leaf on a square of foil. Fold it into a small pocket.
4. Set the pocket beside the candle and light the flame. Sit tall for one minute.
5. Put the pocket in your bag or on your desk. Touch it before quoting a price.
6. If doubt creeps in, repeat the words out loud and stand your ground.

Quick Reminder

Magick does not replace smart action. It powers it. After each spell, do one real-world step: email, call, budget tweak, or application. Small wins compound, and you are building momentum that sticks.

Chapter 3: Bright Studies & Travel Wards

"Learn bright, travel light."

Before my history exam, my hands shook so hard my notes rattled. I drew a tiny Focus Seal in pencil at the corner of my sheet. Tap three times. Inhale four beats. Read one paragraph out loud. The static faded like someone turning down a radio. I finished the test with five minutes to check my answers. Later, on the late bus, I felt that prickle on my neck. Street Shell Ward is small. I pressed my keys in my pocket, pictured a bright shell around me, and named three things I could see. The fear slid back to normal alertness. I got home safe and not frozen.

One history example. Travelers used to wear a St. Christopher medal for safe journeys. The message is simple. Pick a sign that says you are paying attention to your path.

This chapter matters because study and travel both ask for focus and steady nerves. With a few steps, you can turn panic into action and wandering into arrival. If you want your mind present and your feet sure, let's get started.

Exam Panic: Focus Seal

I built this the night before a biology final, hands shaking, flashcards everywhere. I needed a way to quiet the noise and hold one clear goal. I made a ring of sweetness and strength, lit a tiny flame, and felt my heart settle. The answers did not magically appear, but my mind stopped running and finally walked.

WHEN TO PERFORM THIS SPELL:

Wednesday or during a waxing moon

TIME TO ALLOT FOR THE SPELL:

3 minutes

WHERE TO PERFORM THIS SPELL:

Desk or kitchen counter

INGREDIENTS/TOOLS:

- ◊ Small plate
- ◊ Tea light candle
- ◊ Bay leaf
- ◊ Pinch of sugar
- ◊ Pinch of salt

Optional: Add a small rosemary sprig for memory.

Directions

1. On the plate, mix a thin circle of sugar and salt.
2. Place the tea light in the center. Slide the bay leaf under the candle.
3. Hold your hands over the setup and say, "Calm mind, clear sight, steady hand."
4. Light the candle. Breathe in for four counts and out for four counts, three times.
5. Whisper your exam goal once, simple and specific.
6. Snuff the candle. Keep the bay leaf as a bookmark for your notes.

Procrastination Spiral: Task Spark Starter

This one began on a night when my to-do list looked like a monster. I brewed a fast, spiced coffee and charged it with a first step, not a perfect step. The warmth nudged me forward. Ten minutes later, I was already moving.

WHEN TO PERFORM THIS SPELL:

Morning or whenever you feel stuck

TIME TO ALLOT FOR THE SPELL:

3 minutes

WHERE TO PERFORM THIS SPELL:

Kitchen

INGREDIENTS/TOOLS:

◊ Mug

◊ Hot water

◊ Instant coffee

◊ Honey

◊ Ground cinnamon

Optional: Add a pinch of orange zest for sunny drive.

Directions

1. Add instant coffee to your mug. Pour in hot water.
2. Stir clockwise and say, "Start now, small and strong."
3. Add honey and a light dusting of cinnamon.
4. Hold the mug to your chest and name one tiny task you will do first.
5. Take three mindful sips to lock the plan.
6. Set the mug down and begin that one task immediately.

Brain Fog: Clear Head Sweep

I made this after a marathon lecture left my brain in oatmeal mode. A quick lemon and herb rinse over my hands and temples felt like opening a window. The static lifted, and my focus returned.

WHEN TO PERFORM THIS SPELL:

Morning, before class, or during breaks

TIME TO ALLOT FOR THE SPELL:

3 minutes

WHERE TO PERFORM THIS SPELL:

Bathroom or kitchen sink

INGREDIENTS/TOOLS:

◊ Small bowl

◊ Water

◊ Lemon slice

◊ Pinch of salt

◊ Dried rosemary

Optional: Add a peppermint tea bag for extra clarity.

Directions

1. Fill the bowl with water. Squeeze the lemon slice, then drop it in.

2. Add a pinch of salt and a pinch of rosemary.

3. Stir clockwise with your finger and say, "Fog to flow, let clear thought grow."

4. Dip your fingertips and lightly touch your temples and the back of your neck.

5. Cup the water and wash your hands as if rinsing worries away.

6. Air dry your hands for a moment while you breathe steady and visualize a bright, tidy mind.

Time Blindness: Study Block Beacon

This was born from those slippery study sessions that vanish into scrolling. A tiny flame on a bed of rice turned into my time anchor. For three minutes, the world shrank to focus.

WHEN TO PERFORM THIS SPELL:

At the start of every study block

TIME TO ALLOT FOR THE SPELL:

3 minutes

WHERE TO PERFORM THIS SPELL:

Desk

INGREDIENTS/TOOLS:

◊ Heat-safe bowl

◊ Uncooked rice

◊ Tea light candle

◊ Ground cinnamon

◊ Bay leaf

Optional: Add a clove for sharp attention.

Directions

1. Pour a thin layer of rice into the bowl. Nestle the tea light in the center.

2. Place the bay leaf next to the candle. Dust a little cinnamon over the rice.

3. Say, "Beacon bright, hold my sight."

4. Light the candle and focus on a single task until the three minutes pass.

5. When the time is up, snuff the flame and continue for a longer block.

6. Keep the bay leaf under your notebook as your focus token.

Group Challenges: Harmony Weave

I crafted this during a group project that felt like four radios playing at once. Sweetness softened the edges, and spice encouraged action. After a quick shake, our messages landed kinder.

WHEN TO PERFORM THIS SPELL:

Before meetings or when tension rises

TIME TO ALLOT FOR THE SPELL:

3 minutes

WHERE TO PERFORM THIS SPELL:

Desk or kitchen

INGREDIENTS/TOOLS:

- ◊ Small jar with lid
- ◊ Granulated sugar
- ◊ Pinch of salt
- ◊ Ground cinnamon
- ◊ Bay leaf

Optional: Add a drop of vanilla extract for warmth.

Directions

1. Put the bay leaf in the jar. Speak each teammate's name once, kindly.
2. Add two spoonfuls of sugar for sweetness.
3. Add a pinch of salt for protection and clarity.
4. Sprinkle a little cinnamon for momentum.
5. Close the jar and shake gently while saying, "Words soft, work strong."
6. Set the jar near your workspace before your meeting.

Commute Unease: Street Shell Ward

This came from walking home after dark with my shoulders up by my ears. I made a pocket-sized sachet that felt like a small shield. My steps landed steadier.

WHEN TO PERFORM THIS SPELL:

Morning before leaving or right before a comr

TIME TO ALLOT FOR THE SPELL:

3 minutes

WHERE TO PERFORM THIS SPELL:

Kitchen table

INGREDIENTS/TOOLS:

- ◊ Coffee filter
- ◊ Coarse salt
- ◊ Black pepper
- ◊ Whole cloves
- ◊ Kitchen twine

Optional: Add a bay leaf for safe pathways.

Directions

1. Lay the coffee filter flat. Add a spoon of salt, a pinch of pepper, and three cloves.
2. Fold the filter into a little pouch.
3. Tie it closed with twine.
4. Hold it in your palm and say, "Street shell strong, carry me along."
5. Press the sachet to your chest once, then slip it into a pocket or bag.
6. Touch it when you feel uneasy and breathe deep for four counts.

Travel Safety: Safe Seat Charm

I made this before a crowded bus ride that had me on edge. A quick protective oil traced on my shoes and bag made me feel held and alert.

WHEN TO PERFORM THIS SPELL:

Before boarding or getting in a car

TIME TO ALLOT FOR THE SPELL:

3 minutes

WHERE TO PERFORM THIS SPELL:

By the door or at a seat

INGREDIENTS/TOOLS:

◇ Olive oil

◇ Pinch of salt

◇ Dried rosemary

◇ Cotton swab

◇ Tissue

Optional: Add a white tea light at home for a quick blessing.

Directions

1. In your palm, mix a drop of olive oil with a pinch of salt and rosemary.
2. Dip the cotton swab in the blend.
3. Trace a small circle with an X inside on your shoe tips or bag zipper.
4. Say, "Safe seat, safe road, safe return."
5. Wipe excess oil with the tissue.
6. Step out feeling grounded and aware.

Lost Items or Luggage: Return Tag Spell

I made this after a suitcase went on its own vacation. A floating leaf and a small flame became my homing beacon. The bag showed up soon after, and I have used this simple pull ever since.

WHEN TO PERFORM THIS SPELL:

As soon as you notice something is missing

TIME TO ALLOT FOR THE SPELL:

3 minutes

WHERE TO PERFORM THIS SPELL:

Table or nightstand

INGREDIENTS/TOOLS:

- ◊ Small bowl
- ◊ Water
- ◊ Bay leaf
- ◊ Granulated sugar
- ◊ Tea light candle

Optional: Add a pinch of coffee grounds to energize the search.

Directions

1. Fill the bowl with water and place it in front of you.
2. Hold the bay leaf and whisper what should return.
3. Float the bay leaf on the water. Sprinkle a little sugar toward it to attract.
4. Say, "What is mine returns to me."
5. Light the tea light and focus on the item for one minute.
6. Snuff the candle. Leave the bowl out until the item is found.

Unfamiliar Spaces: Fresh Sweep Claiming

First nights in new dorms and hotels can feel like sleeping in a stranger's shoes. A quick citrus wipe claims the room for your energy. The whole place breathes easier.

WHEN TO PERFORM THIS SPELL:

Right after arriving in a new space

TIME TO ALLOT FOR THE SPELL:

3 minutes

WHERE TO PERFORM THIS SPELL:

Room doorway and main surfaces

INGREDIENTS/TOOLS:

- ◊ White vinegar
- ◊ Water
- ◊ Lemon peel
- ◊ Pinch of salt
- ◊ Paper towels

Optional: Add a few lavender buds for soft peace.

Directions

1. Mix a splash of vinegar with water on a folded paper towel.
2. Add a little salt to the towel and rub in a strip of lemon peel.
3. Wipe the door handle and door frame from top to bottom.
4. Say, "I claim this room for rest and good work."
5. Lightly wipe your desk and the bedside surface.
6. Open a window or imagine fresh air sweeping through.

Travel Anxiety: Sky Calm Press

This one came from a bumpy flight where my breath went shallow. I built a quick anchor you can do in your seat. Sweet, steady, and simple.

WHEN TO PERFORM THIS SPELL:

Before takeoff or when nerves rise

TIME TO ALLOT FOR THE SPELL:

3 minutes

WHERE TO PERFORM THIS SPELL:

Airport seat or plane seat

INGREDIENTS/TOOLS:

- ◇ Peppermint candy or gum
- ◇ Water bottle
- ◇ Sugar packet
- ◇ Salt packet
- ◇ Cotton string or kitchen twine

Optional: Add a chamomile tea bag to hold and breathe in its scent.

Directions

1. Tie the string around your wrist with three gentle loops. With each loop say, "In," "Out," "Calm."
2. Place the peppermint candy in your mouth for steady, cool breathing.
3. Add a tiny pinch of sugar and salt to a sip of water.
4. Sip slowly and imagine your heartbeat smoothing out.
5. Press the string knot lightly with your thumb for ten breaths.
6. Keep the string on until you land or arrive, then untie and thank your journey.

Use these like pocket tools. Short, simple, and ready when you are. Keep going, bright traveler.

Chapter 4 Sacred Friends & Family

"Hold your center; mend the thread."

My roommate and I were fighting about dishes, but really we were scared and tired. The sink smelled like old noodles. I drew a small Flow Pact mark under the counter edge. We sat with a timer for ten minutes and wrote the jobs we each could own. Tuesdays for trash. Music off after ten. A code word for I need quiet. We both signed the paper with the same blue pen. The kitchen felt lighter, like someone opened a window. A week later, a friend repeated a rumor about me. My jaw burned. I used Mirrorback Deflection. I pictured a clean mirror between us and said, I do not accept that story. Please bring me the source or drop it. My voice stayed low. The rumor died.

One history example. In Ireland, people weave a Brigid's cross and hang it near the door for blessing and house peace. It is humble straw, but it works like a promise to keep the home safe.

This chapter matters because relationships are built in tiny choices. Clear jobs, gentle truth, and quick repairs save love from slow damage. If you want home to feel like a place you help keep, not a storm you hide from, let's get started.

Roommate Tension - Flow Pact

I made this when the sink looked like a museum of dirty plates and no one would admit it. I turned on the lamp, set a tiny candle on a saucer, and dabbed it with olive oil like I was blessing a peace treaty. The room felt less sharp. I didn't need a speech. I needed calm in my chest so I could ask for help without sparks.

WHEN TO PERFORM THIS SPELL:

On a Saturday or during a waning moon

TIME TO ALLOT FOR THE SPELL:

3 minutes

WHERE TO PERFORM THE SPELL:

Kitchen sink or counter

INGREDIENTS/TOOLS:

- ◊ White vinegar
- ◊ Table salt
- ◊ Olive oil
- ◊ Bay leaf
- ◊ Small white candle

Optional: Add a pinch of dried rosemary.

Directions

1. Put the candle on a plate. Rub a drop of olive oil on it from base to top.

2. Sprinkle salt in a small ring around the candle.

3. Dip two fingers in vinegar. Smooth a line of vinegar along the sink faucet or dish area.

4. Hold the bay leaf near your heart and say, "Let our space flow. Let our care grow."

5. Light the candle for a minute while you breathe. Then pinch it out. Safety first.

Friendship Drift - Thread-Stitch Repair

After months of silence with a close friend, I brewed tea and stirred like I was stitching something invisible. Honey for softness, lemon for fresh starts. I sent one honest text. The thread caught. We found our way back by talking about small things first.

WHEN TO PERFORM THIS SPELL:

On a Friday or during a new moon

TIME TO ALLOT FOR THE SPELL:

3 minutes

WHERE TO PERFORM THE SPELL:

Kitchen table

INGREDIENTS/TOOLS:

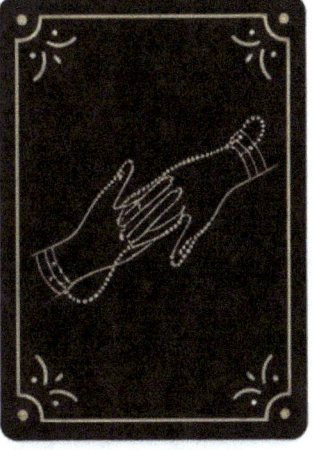

- ◇ Black tea bag
- ◇ Honey
- ◇ Cinnamon
- ◇ Lemon slice
- ◇ Sugar

Optional: Add rose petals.

Directions

1. Brew the tea. Add a pinch of cinnamon and a fingertip of sugar.
2. Squeeze the lemon slice, then add a ribbon of honey.
3. Stir clockwise and say, "What frayed returns with care."
4. Sip slowly. When you feel ready, send a simple check-in message.

Unwanted Questions – Shield Fold

My aunt could pry secrets from a stone. Before dinner, I made a tiny packet that felt like armor in my pocket. When the probing started, I smiled and redirected. The questions slid off like rain on a coat.

WHEN TO PERFORM THIS SPELL:

Before a visit or during a waning moon

TIME TO ALLOT FOR THE SPELL:

3 minutes

WHERE TO PERFORM THE SPELL:

Kitchen counter

INGREDIENTS/TOOLS:

- ◊ Aluminum foil
- ◊ Bay leaf
- ◊ Salt
- ◊ Black pepper
- ◊ Coffee grounds

Optional: Add a whole clove.

Directions

1. Place a small square of foil shiny side out.
2. Set the bay leaf in the center. Add a pinch of salt, pepper, and coffee grounds.
3. Fold the foil into a neat packet. Hold it to your chest and say, "My edges are mine."
4. Keep it in your pocket during the conversation.

Homesickness - Hearth-Spark Comfort

There was a winter night when I missed home so hard my bones ached. I made cinnamon toast the way my dad did, and the first bite cracked something warm open. I wasn't alone. The taste was a doorway.

WHEN TO PERFORM THIS SPELL:

On a Sunday or any chilly evening

TIME TO ALLOT FOR THE SPELL:

3 minutes

WHERE TO PERFORM THE SPELL:

Kitchen

INGREDIENTS/TOOLS:

- ◊ **Bread**
- ◊ **Butter**
- ◊ **Cinnamon**
- ◊ **Sugar**
- ◊ **Vanilla extract**

Optional: Add a pinch of nutmeg.

Directions

1. Toast the bread. Mix a little sugar and cinnamon.

2. Butter the toast. Sprinkle the cinnamon sugar. Touch the bread and say, "Home lives in me."

3. Dab a drop of vanilla on the plate. Inhale the scent, then eat slowly.

Loneliness New Places - Open-Door Charm

When I moved to a new city, the quiet felt way too loud. I mixed a simple threshold charm and flicked it across my doorway. The next week, I found myself saying yes to a coffee invite without overthinking. The world felt more open.

WHEN TO PERFORM THIS SPELL:

On a Thursday or during a waxing moon

TIME TO ALLOT FOR THE SPELL:

3 minutes

WHERE TO PERFORM THE SPELL:

Front door threshold

INGREDIENTS/TOOLS:

⋄ White vinegar

⋄ Lemon

⋄ Sugar

⋄ Salt

⋄ Bay leaf

Optional: Add dried basil.

Directions

1. In a cup, mix a splash of vinegar with a squeeze of lemon. Add a pinch of sugar and salt.

2. Hold the bay leaf over the cup and say, "Kind faces find me."

3. Dip your fingers and flick three drops outside and three inside your doorway.

4. Tuck the bay leaf above the door frame if you can.

Gossip Swirl - Mirrorback Deflection

I felt the sting of whispers I wasn't meant to hear. I made a tiny mirror charm and the spiral lost its pull. The talk kept moving, but it didn't stick to me anymore.

WHEN TO PERFORM THIS SPELL:

On a Wednesday or during a waning moon

TIME TO ALLOT FOR THE SPELL:

3 minutes

WHERE TO PERFORM THE SPELL:

Kitchen or near a window

INGREDIENTS/TOOLS:

- ◊ Aluminum foil
- ◊ Salt
- ◊ Black pepper
- ◊ Sugar
- ◊ Bay leaf

Optional: Add a few sesame seeds for luck.

Directions

1. Cut a small square of foil, shiny side out.
2. Place the bay leaf on it. Add a pinch of salt for purity, sugar for sweetness, and pepper for protection.
3. Fold the foil so the shiny side faces outward like a mirror.
4. Hold it up and say, "What is not mine reflects away."
5. Carry in your bag or tape it behind a picture frame.

Boundary Guilt – Grace Seal

Saying no used to leave me shaky. I started sealing my voice with a warm sip that steadied my heart. I could decline without apologizing for existing.

WHEN TO PERFORM THIS SPELL:

Before a tough talk or on a Tuesday

TIME TO ALLOT FOR THE SPELL:

3 minutes

WHERE TO PERFORM THE SPELL:

Kitchen

INGREDIENTS/TOOLS:

- ◊ Chamomile tea bag
- ◊ Lemon
- ◊ Honey
- ◊ Cinnamon
- ◊ Salt

Optional: Add ginger powder.

Directions

1. Brew chamomile. Add a squeeze of lemon and a dot of honey.
2. Sprinkle a tiny pinch of cinnamon and the smallest grain of salt.
3. Hold the cup at your throat and say, "My no is kind and clear."
4. Sip. Then send the text or speak the sentence.

Holiday Anxiety - Peace-Path Prep

Before big gatherings, my chest could buzz like a beehive. I brewed peppermint and breathed with the steam. The room softened. I walked in with steadier feet.

WHEN TO PERFORM THIS SPELL:

Morning of the event or on a Friday

TIME TO ALLOT FOR THE SPELL:

3 minutes

WHERE TO PERFORM THE SPELL:

Kitchen or by a window

INGREDIENTS/TOOLS:

◊ **Peppermint tea bag**

◊ **Honey**

◊ **Vanilla extract**

◊ **Cinnamon**

◊ **Salt**

 Optional: Add orange peel.

Directions

1. Brew peppermint. Stir in a touch of honey and a drop of vanilla.
2. Add a whisper of cinnamon and a single grain of salt.
3. Cup the steam and say, "I choose peace in each step."
4. Drink, then map your exit plan and one safe topic.

Family Spats – Bridge Ease

We kept snapping over nothing. I tore a piece of bread, dipped it in oil, and named what I actually wanted. Calm slipped back in. We found the bridge between us.

WHEN TO PERFORM THIS SPELL:

Before a talk or on a Sunday

TIME TO ALLOT FOR THE SPELL:

3 minutes

WHERE TO PERFORM THE SPELL:

Kitchen table

INGREDIENTS/TOOLS:

◊ Bread

◊ Olive oil

◊ Salt

◊ Black pepper

◊ Small white candle

Optional: Add dried thyme.

Directions

1. Pour a little oil into a small dish. Sprinkle salt and pepper on top.

2. Light the candle. Break the bread into two pieces.

3. Dip one piece in the oil. Say, "I cross with care. Let peace meet me."

4. Eat the dipped piece. Save the second to share or crumble outside as an offering.

5. Blow out the candle. Never leave it unattended.

Rebuilding Trust – Tower Stonework

After a hard break in a relationship, I built a small tower in a glass. Layer by layer, I spoke what I could repair. It wasn't instant. But the daily sight of it kept me steady. Brick by brick, we tried again with truth.

WHEN TO PERFORM THIS SPELL:

On a Monday or during a waxing moon

TIME TO ALLOT FOR THE SPELL:

4 minutes

WHERE TO PERFORM THE SPELL:

Kitchen counter or windowsill

INGREDIENTS/TOOLS:

◊ Rice

◊ Sugar

◊ Salt

◊ Coffee grounds

◊ Honey

Optional: Add a bay leaf on top.

Directions

1. In a clear glass, pour a thin layer of rice. Say, "Foundation."

2. Add a layer of sugar. Say, "Good faith."

3. Add a thin ring of salt. Say, "Boundaries."

4. Sprinkle coffee grounds. Say, "Awake and honest."

5. Drizzle a little honey on top. Say, "May trust return with care."

6. Set the tower where you will see it. When you both reach a milestone, dissolve the contents in warm water and pour it down the sink to release the past.

Chapter 5: Gentle Health & Healing

"Your body is an ally."

I could not sleep. My room was clean and still felt loud. I made Pillow Drift. I filled a small cloth square with chamomile and a pinch of salt, tied it with red thread, and breathed a slow count on each knot. I tucked it into my pillowcase and told my body, We can rest now. That first night I did not conk out. I just stopped fighting. The next night, I fell asleep halfway through a page of my book. On a bad afternoon, my chest buzzed like a beehive. Ground Anchor helped. I stood with bare feet on the tile, pressed my palm to my belly, and named five heavy things in the room. Table. Books. Pot. Door. Floor. My breath thickened in a good way. The room came back into focus.

One history example. In the healing temples of Asklepios, people slept to invite helpful dreams. It was not magic in a movie sense. It was rest plus meaning.

This chapter matters because your body is not a machine you can shame into working. It is a place you live. These small acts teach your nervous system what safety feels like. If you want rest to be reachable and calm to be a skill, let's get started.

Insomnia Loop: Pillow Drift

I first made this spell on a night when my brain felt like a TV with the volume stuck too loud. I warmed a mug in my hands, breathed in the soft apple-sweet scent of chamomile, and let the honey melt like a slow sunset. With each sip, my shoulders dropped. The steam felt like a hush over my thoughts. I drifted, not from force, but because my body finally felt safe to.

WHEN TO PERFORM THIS SPELL:

Nighttime, especially during a waning moon

TIME TO ALLOT FOR THE SPELL:

3 minutes

WHERE TO PERFORM THE SPELL:

Kitchen, then bedside

INGREDIENTS/TOOLS:

- ◊ Mug
- ◊ Hot water
- ◊ Chamomile tea bag
- ◊ Honey
- ◊ Ground cinnamon

Optional: Add vanilla extract. Not required, but adds an extra layer of energy.

Directions

1. Rinse the mug with hot water to warm it.
2. Steep the chamomile for 1 minute. Add honey and a pinch of cinnamon.
3. Hold the mug at heart level and say, "I release the day. My mind rests. My body keeps me."
4. Sip slowly. Between sips, count 4 in, 6 out.
5. Leave a tiny cooled sip on the nightstand as a "rest offering," then sleep.

Nightmares: Star Ward

The first time I made this, I was tired of waking up in a sweat. I filled a tiny bag with rice and spice, sealed it like a secret, and set a candle for one steady minute. That night, my dreams felt guarded, like a friend standing watch at my door.

WHEN TO PERFORM THIS SPELL:

Evening, Friday or Saturday

TIME TO ALLOT FOR THE SPELL:

3 minutes

WHERE TO PERFORM THE SPELL:

Kitchen, then under or beside your pillow

INGREDIENTS/TOOLS:

- ◊ Zip-top sandwich bag
- ◊ Uncooked rice
- ◊ Cinnamon stick or pinch
- ◊ Chamomile tea bag
- ◊ White tealight candle

Optional: Add a pinch of cocoa powder. Not required, but adds an extra layer of energy.

Directions

1. Place rice, chamomile, and cinnamon into the zip bag. Press out air and seal.
2. Hold the bag between palms and say, "Stars watch. Dreams wash. I sleep in peace."
3. Light the tealight for 1 minute to "charge" the bag. Blow it out. Never sleep with a candle lit.
4. Slip the bag under the pillow corner or on the nightstand.
5. If you wake from a bad dream, grip the bag, breathe 4 slow cycles, and return to sleep.

Sick-Day Blues: Soothe Charm

I brewed this on a rainy cold when my voice sounded like gravel. The steam hugged my face, the ginger warmed my chest, and the lemon felt like a small sun. I didn't need to power through. I needed to soften.

WHEN TO PERFORM THIS SPELL:

Any sick day, morning or afternoon

TIME TO ALLOT FOR THE SPELL:

4 minutes

WHERE TO PERFORM THE SPELL:

Kitchen

INGREDIENTS/TOOLS:

◊ Mug

◊ Hot water

◊ Fresh ginger slices or ground ginger

◊ Lemon slice

◊ Honey

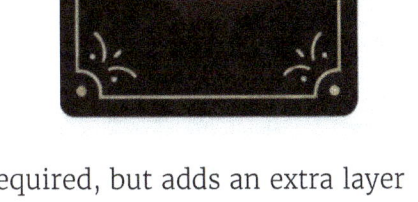

Optional: Add a pinch of turmeric. Not required, but adds an extra layer of energy.

Directions

1. Steep ginger in hot water for 2 minutes.

2. Add lemon and honey. Stir clockwise and say, "Warmth in, ache out. Comfort finds me."

3. Hold the mug under your nose and take 3 steam breaths, eyes closed.

4. Sip slowly. With each swallow, imagine warmth spreading through your chest and throat.

5. Rest. That is the spell finishing its work.

Anxiety Spike: Ground Anchor

The first time I felt panic creeping up, I went to the sink. Salt, water, cold, breath. Simple things. They pulled me back into my body like a rope.

WHEN TO PERFORM THIS SPELL:

Anytime a wave hits

TIME TO ALLOT FOR THE SPELL:

3 to 5 minutes

WHERE TO PERFORM THE SPELL:

Kitchen sink or counter

INGREDIENTS/TOOLS:

- ◊ Glass of cool water
- ◊ Pinch of salt
- ◊ Ice cube
- ◊ Paper napkin or towel
- ◊ White tealight candle

Optional: Add a bay leaf to hold. Not required, but adds an extra layer of energy.

Directions

1. Place the tealight on the counter and light it. Focus on the steady flame.

2. Put a tiny pinch of salt on your tongue. Sip water to dissolve. Say, "I am here."

3. Hold the ice cube wrapped in the napkin to your wrist for 30 seconds. Count out loud: 1 to 30.

4. Breathe 4 in, hold 4, breathe 6 out. Repeat 4 times.

5. Blow out the candle to seal. Press palms on the counter and feel the surface hold you.

Burnout: Restore Pause Ritual

I built this on a week when everything felt like a checklist. The thyme steam lifted the mental fog, the lemon cut the heaviness, and the quiet minute felt like plugging myself back in.

WHEN TO PERFORM THIS SPELL:

Late afternoon or Sunday evening

TIME TO ALLOT FOR THE SPELL:

12 minutes

WHERE TO PERFORM THE SPELL:

Kitchen table or sink

INGREDIENTS/TOOLS:

- ◇ Kettle or small pot
- ◇ Hot water
- ◇ Dried thyme
- ◇ Lemon slice
- ◇ White candle

Optional: Add a pinch of sea salt to the steam. Not required, but adds an extra layer of energy.

Directions

1. Place 1 teaspoon thyme and the lemon slice in a heat-safe bowl.

2. Pour hot water over. Tent your head with a towel if you like and inhale steam for 3 minutes.

3. Light the candle. Sit with eyes closed and say, "I pause. I refill. I return whole."

4. List three tasks you release until tomorrow, silently.

5. Snuff the candle. Pour the cooled thyme water down the drain as the burnout washes away.

Head Tension: Quiet-Crown Ease

One afternoon my forehead felt tight, like a headband cinched too hard. A cool peppermint compress and a breath count loosened the grip.

WHEN TO PERFORM THIS SPELL:

At the first sign of tension

TIME TO ALLOT FOR THE SPELL:

8 minutes

WHERE TO PERFORM THE SPELL:

Kitchen, then a quiet chair

INGREDIENTS/TOOLS:

- ◇ Peppermint tea bag
- ◇ Hot water
- ◇ Ice cube
- ◇ Pinch of salt
- ◇ Paper towel

Optional: Add a strip of lemon peel to the steep. Not required, but adds an extra layer of energy.

Directions

1. Steep the tea bag in hot water for 2 minutes, then add the ice to cool it to lukewarm.

2. Sprinkle a tiny pinch of salt into the tea to ground the mind.

3. Soak the paper towel, wring lightly, and place across your forehead.

4. Breathe in 4, out 7 for 3 minutes. Whisper, "Ease at my crown."

5. Repeat once if needed. Sip a little of the cooled tea to finish.

Body Neutrality Wobble: Kind Mirror

On a day when the mirror felt unfriendly, I used a spoon instead. The soft reflection looked like a watercolor version of me, kinder and real. I could meet my own eyes without picking myself apart.

WHEN TO PERFORM THIS SPELL:

Morning or pre-shower

TIME TO ALLOT FOR THE SPELL:

6 minutes

WHERE TO PERFORM THE SPELL:

Kitchen

INGREDIENTS/TOOLS:

- ◇ Clean metal spoon
- ◇ Glass of warm water
- ◇ Honey
- ◇ Ground cinnamon
- ◇ White tealight candle

Optional: Add a strawberry slice for sweetness. Not required, but adds an extra layer of energy.

Directions

1. Stir a fingertip of honey and a tiny pinch of cinnamon into the warm water.
2. Light the candle. Hold the spoon as a mirror.
3. Sip the sweet water and say, "I am more than a look. I am living."
4. Look into the spoon. Name 3 things your body did for you today.
5. Blow out the candle. Keep the spoon on the counter as a gentle reminder.

Shallow Breathing: Triangle-Calm Pattern

I tried this during a shaky moment. Three beans became my triangle, and tracing their edges slowed my breath until my chest stopped fluttering.

WHEN TO PERFORM THIS SPELL:

Anytime breath feels choppy

TIME TO ALLOT FOR THE SPELL:

4 minutes

WHERE TO PERFORM THE SPELL:

Kitchen table

INGREDIENTS/TOOLS:

- ◇ 3 dried beans
- ◇ Small plate
- ◇ Glass of water
- ◇ Peppermint tea bag or mint candy
- ◇ White candle

Optional: Add a pinch of sugar to symbolize steady energy. Not required, but adds an extra layer of energy.

Directions

1. Place the beans on the plate as a triangle. Light the candle.
2. Touch each bean with your finger while breathing: side one 3 counts in, side two 3 counts hold, side three 4 counts out.
3. Repeat 6 triangles.
4. Sip water and let a bit of peppermint open your chest.
5. Blow out the candle. Pocket the beans as calm tokens.

Pain Overwhelm: Ease-Within Pocket Spell

On a rough flare day, I needed comfort I could carry. I packed a tiny bundle that felt like a steady heartbeat in my palm.

WHEN TO PERFORM THIS SPELL:

Morning or at the start of a flare

TIME TO ALLOT FOR THE SPELL:

5 minutes

WHERE TO PERFORM THE SPELL:

Kitchen counter

INGREDIENTS/TOOLS:

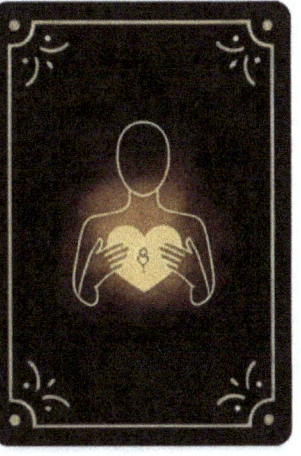

- ◊ Uncooked rice
- ◊ Bay leaf
- ◊ Chamomile tea bag or loose chamomile
- ◊ Pinch of salt
- ◊ Square of aluminum foil

Optional: Add a clove for gentle numbing energy. Not required, but adds an extra layer of energy.

Directions

1. Place a tablespoon of rice on the foil. Add the chamomile and salt.

2. Gently etch a tiny line or heart into the bay leaf with your fingernail. Place it on top.

3. Fold the foil into a small packet. Hold it between palms and say, "Ease within me. Pain, soften."

4. Keep it in your pocket. When overwhelmed, squeeze and breathe 5 slow breaths.

5. Replace the packet weekly. Dispose by opening and sprinkling contents into soil or trash with thanks.

Morning Slump: Momentum Brew

I made this on a gray Monday. The citrus woke the room. The cinnamon felt like a drumbeat. By the time I set the mug down, I had enough spark to begin.

WHEN TO PERFORM THIS SPELL:

Early morning

TIME TO ALLOT FOR THE SPELL:

6 minutes

WHERE TO PERFORM THE SPELL:

Kitchen

INGREDIENTS/TOOLS:

◊ Mug

◊ Hot brewed coffee or black tea

◊ Orange or lemon peel

◊ Honey

◊ Ground cinnamon

Optional: Add a pinch of cacao powder. Not required, but adds an extra layer of energy.

Directions

1. Add a strip of citrus peel and a pinch of cinnamon to your hot coffee or tea.

2. Stir in honey. Hold the mug with both hands and say, "Spark to start. I move with purpose."

3. Take 3 strong breaths with the mug under your nose.

4. Sip mindfully. With each sip, picture your first task getting done.

5. Leave the peel on the saucer as a small sun for your day.

Chapter 6: Everyday Protection & Boundaries

"Ward first, wander later."

I said yes to every message and wondered why I felt hollow. One night I drew a thin salt line at my front door and spoke my house rules out loud. Then I set DM Gatekeeper on my phone. I wrote one sentence for strangers. Thank you for reaching out. I will reply in work hours. I put the sentence in a note and pasted it when I needed it. The change felt almost physical. My room seemed taller. The quiet after 9 p.m. felt like warm water.

One history example. In old houses, people hid witch bottles under floors. They filled them with pins and hair to catch harm before it crossed the threshold. It was a simple boundary you could point to.

This chapter matters because kindness without edges turns into sleep deprivation and resentment. Boundaries are not walls. They are doors that you can open and close on purpose. If you want your time and space to feel safe and yours, let's get started.

Nosy Neighbors: Doorway Drift Ward

For privacy in shared spaces.

I made this ward the week a neighbor kept pausing at my door to "just check in." Every sound in the hall made my shoulders jump. I set a tiny bowl by the threshold, and as the candle warmed the spices, the air felt less nosy and more mine. That night the hallway chatter faded like a radio turning down. My door felt like a quiet, anchored island.

WHEN TO PERFORM THIS SPELL:

Any morning or Saturday

TIME TO ALLOT FOR THE SPELL:

3 minutes

WHERE TO PERFORM THE SPELL:

Front door or main entry

INGREDIENTS/TOOLS:

◇ Small heat-safe bowl

◇ Coarse salt

◇ Ground black pepper

◇ Bay leaf

◇ White tea light candle

Optional: Add a pinch of dried rosemary. Not required, but adds an extra layer of energy.

Directions

1. Crack a window for airflow. Place the unlit candle and bowl at your door.
2. Pour a layer of salt into the bowl, then a light dusting of pepper.
3. Light the candle. Never leave it unattended.
4. Hold the bay leaf over the flame's heat, then trace a small circle in the air at the doorway.
5. Set the leaf upright in the salt and say, "This door is mine, my peace defined."
6. Let the candle burn for a minute, then snuff it. Keep the bowl by the door for 24 hours, then toss the contents outside or into the trash.

Leaky Energy: Bubble Perimeter

For keeping your aura contained.

I tried this quick bubble the day I felt like a sponge soaking up other people's moods. After a drop of oil and a pinch of salt, I could almost hear an inner click, like a space suit sealing. The swirl of other folks' feelings stayed outside. I kept my own center.

WHEN TO PERFORM THIS SPELL:

Before leaving home or before a call

TIME TO ALLOT FOR THE SPELL:

3 minutes

WHERE TO PERFORM THE SPELL:

Kitchen counter or bathroom sink

INGREDIENTS/TOOLS:

- ◊ Small bowl
- ◊ Water
- ◊ Table salt
- ◊ Olive oil
- ◊ White tea light candle

 Optional: Add a pinch of dried basil for calm confidence.

Directions

1. Fill the bowl with water. Add a pinch of salt and one drop of olive oil.
2. Swirl clockwise with your fingertip while breathing deep.
3. Light the candle. Hold the bowl so the surface shimmers in the light.
4. Touch a dab of the water to your forehead, chest, and wrists.
5. Say, "Clear and whole, I keep my soul."
6. Snuff the candle. Pour the remaining water down the sink.

Energy Vampires: Thread Severance

For cutting draining ties.

I used this when a constant complainer kept parking their storm cloud over my day. I tied the string, named the weight, and broke it. The moment the twine snapped, my body felt lighter, like dropping a heavy backpack I forgot I was carrying.

WHEN TO PERFORM THIS SPELL:

Sunset or after a tiring interaction

TIME TO ALLOT FOR THE SPELL:

3 minutes

WHERE TO PERFORM THE SPELL:

Kitchen table with a plate

INGREDIENTS/TOOLS:

◊ **Kitchen twine**

◊ **Small plate**

◊ **Table salt**

◊ **Lemon**

◊ **White tea light candle**

Optional: Add a sprinkle of ground clove for extra cut-and-clear strength.

Directions

1. Place the plate on the table and coil a short length of twine on it.

2. Tie a simple knot and quietly name what it represents.

3. Sprinkle a pinch of salt over the knot to purify.

4. Light the candle. Squeeze a drop of lemon juice onto the knot.

5. Hold the knot near the candle's warmth and say, "What drains me ends. My energy mends."

6. Snap the twine by hand to sever the tie. Toss twine and lemon into the trash and snuff the candle.

Rumors: Mirror Return Spell

For gossip that needs deflecting.

When whispers started repeating my life back to me with edits, I built a tiny mirror out of foil, honey, and spice. It reflected the mess away while sweetening the air. The echo died down, and my name felt like mine again.

WHEN TO PERFORM THIS SPELL:

Morning on a Wednesday or any time rumors

TIME TO ALLOT FOR THE SPELL:

3 minutes

WHERE TO PERFORM THE SPELL:

Kitchen counter

INGREDIENTS/TOOLS:

- ◇ Aluminum foil square
- ◇ Honey
- ◇ Ground cinnamon
- ◇ Small bowl of water
- ◇ White tea light candle

Optional: Add a pinch of sugar for extra sweetness.

Directions

1. Lay the foil shiny side up like a pocket mirror.
2. Dab a tiny bit of honey in the center, then dust with cinnamon.
3. Light the candle and pass the foil through the warm air above the flame.
4. Hold the foil at chest level and say, "Words that stray, reflect away."
5. Touch a corner of the foil to the water to cool and seal.
6. Fold the foil shut and tuck it in a wallet or near your door. Snuff the candle.

Bedroom Unease: Night-Watch Water Guard

For restless feelings in your own space.

I made this the week my room felt jumpy for no reason. The glass by the bed drank up the static while I slept. I woke up clearer, as if the night had rinsed the walls.

WHEN TO PERFORM THIS SPELL:

Right before bedtime

TIME TO ALLOT FOR THE SPELL:

3 minutes

WHERE TO PERFORM THE SPELL:

Nightstand

INGREDIENTS/TOOLS:

◇ Clear glass

◇ Water

◇ Table salt

◇ Chamomile tea bag

◇ Uncooked rice

Optional: Add a pinch of dried lavender for deeper calm.

Directions

1. Fill the glass with water and add a small pinch of salt.
2. Drop in three grains of rice for steadiness.
3. Hold the chamomile tea bag over the glass so its scent brushes the water.
4. Say, "Through this night, keep me light."
5. Set the glass on your nightstand. Do not drink it.
6. In the morning, pour the water down the sink and toss the rice and tea bag.

Heavy Thresholds: Salt Sweep

For clearing entryways of stagnant energy.

I used this after the house felt like it was holding its breath. A quick sprinkle, a steady count, a lift into the trash, and the doorway felt brighter. Even the floor seemed to exhale.

WHEN TO PERFORM THIS SPELL:

Morning or right after cleaning

TIME TO ALLOT FOR THE SPELL:

3 minutes

WHERE TO PERFORM THE SPELL:

Front or back door threshold

INGREDIENTS/TOOLS:

◊ Table salt

◊ Dry rice

◊ Lemon

◊ Ground black pepper

◊ Paper towel

Optional: Add a pinch of baking soda for extra freshness.

Directions

1. Mix a pinch of salt, a pinch of rice, and a light shake of pepper in your palm.

2. Sprinkle a thin line across the threshold.

3. Count slowly to nine while visualizing a clear, bright doorway.

4. Rub a small piece of lemon peel between your fingers and swipe it along the threshold.

5. Use the paper towel to gather the sprinkle into your hand.

6. Toss it into the trash and say, "Only welcome feet, cross this street."

Workplace Negativity: Desk Shield

For protecting your focus and energy.

I built this jar after a week of sighs, side-eyes, and meetings that went nowhere. The moment I sealed it and gave it a shake, my desk felt like a little lighthouse. The noise kept breaking on the glass and rolling away.

WHEN TO PERFORM THIS SPELL:

Start of the workday or after lunch

TIME TO ALLOT FOR THE SPELL:

3 minutes

WHERE TO PERFORM THIS SPELL:

Desk at home or the break room

INGREDIENTS/TOOLS:

- ◊ Small jar with lid
- ◊ Coffee grounds
- ◊ Ground cinnamon
- ◊ Dried rosemary
- ◊ Table salt

Optional: Add a bay leaf tucked inside the lid.

Directions

1. Add a teaspoon of coffee grounds to the jar for alertness.
2. Add a pinch of cinnamon for warmth and respect.
3. Add a pinch of dried rosemary for mental clarity.
4. Add a tiny pinch of salt to seal the blend.
5. Close the lid and shake gently while saying, "Focus stays, stray noise strays."
6. Keep the jar on your desk. Refresh monthly.

Phone Overreach: DM Gatekeeper

For digital boundaries and unwanted messages.

I made this bowl after late-night DMs kept poking holes in my peace. Sweet met sour, and my screen felt less grabby. The pings stopped feeling like hooks and more like gentle taps I could answer on my time.

WHEN TO PERFORM THIS SPELL:

Before opening messages or at sunset

TIME TO ALLOT FOR THE SPELL:

3 minutes

WHERE TO PERFORM THIS SPELL:

Kitchen counter

INGREDIENTS/TOOLS:

- ◊ Small bowl
- ◊ White vinegar
- ◊ Sugar
- ◊ Bay leaf
- ◊ White tea light candle

Optional: Add a pinch of vanilla for kinder tones online.

Directions

1. Pour a tablespoon of vinegar into the bowl. Add a teaspoon of sugar and swirl until it blends.

2. Light the candle.

3. Hold the bay leaf over the bowl and whisper what you allow and what you do not.

4. Dip the tip of the leaf in the sweet-sour mix to seal your words.

5. Say, "My time, my gate. Your wait can wait."

6. Tuck the dry leaf near your phone charger or case. Snuff the candle.

Password Anxiety: Sentinel Charm

For safe logins and online protection.

I made this sachet the night I kept second-guessing every password. Knot by knot, my nerves settled. I tied it and felt a calm guard dog sit by my keyboard.

WHEN TO PERFORM THIS SPELL:

Before changing passwords or starting a new

TIME TO ALLOT FOR THE SPELL:

3 minutes

WHERE TO PERFORM THIS SPELL:

Kitchen table

INGREDIENTS/TOOLS:

- ◊ Coffee filter
- ◊ Table salt
- ◊ Dried rosemary
- ◊ Whole black peppercorns
- ◊ Kitchen twine

 Optional: Add a pinch of dried lemon zest for clarity.

Directions

1. Set the coffee filter flat. Add a teaspoon of salt.
2. Add a pinch of rosemary and three peppercorns.
3. Gather the filter's edges to form a pouch.
4. Tie closed with twine, making three firm knots.
5. Hold the sachet to your chest and say, "Guard my keys. Keep them, please."
6. Place it near your router or keyboard. Replace every three months.

After-Conflict Residue: Peace Diffuser

For calming energy after arguments.

I simmered this after a sharp conversation still buzzed in the room. As the steam lifted lemon and spice, the edges of the moment softened. The air felt like it forgave the day.

WHEN TO PERFORM THIS SPELL:

Right after an argument or at dusk

TIME TO ALLOT FOR THE SPELL:

3 minutes active, then let it simmer

WHERE TO PERFORM THIS SPELL:

Stove top

INGREDIENTS/TOOLS:

◊ Small pot

◊ Water

◊ Lemon slices

◊ Ground cinnamon

◊ Vanilla extract

Optional: Add a sprig of fresh mint for harmony.

Directions

1. Fill the pot with a cup of water. Add two lemon slices.
2. Sprinkle a pinch of cinnamon and a few drops of vanilla.
3. Bring to a gentle simmer.
4. Stand safely by the steam and breathe slowly.
5. Say, "Peace returns. Heat now turns."
6. Turn off the heat. Let it cool, then pour down the sink.

Quick Tip: Protection is upkeep. Small, regular wards do more than one big scramble when things go sideways. Choose a favorite and make it a habit.

Chapter 7: Serene Mental Calm & Forgiveness

"Let go without letting yourself go."

My thoughts used to gallop until I felt sick. The first time I tried Quiet Mind Aegis, I sat on the carpet and touched my forehead with two fingers. I breathed in through my nose and out through my mouth. I pictured a thin glass lid closing over a cup of water. Thoughts still moved under the glass, but they stopped splashing out. Later, when I messed up with a friend, the shame felt like wet cement. Done is Good saved me. I set a five minute timer and wrote a simple apology that owned my part and did not ask for comfort. I sent it. My stomach unclenched. I could act again.

One history example. Monks used prayer beads to count slow breaths. The tool is tiny, but it gives your mind something steady to hold.

This chapter matters because a loud mind steals whole days. Calm is not silence. Calm is the power to choose your next move. If you want your thoughts to be your helpers, not your captains, let's get started

Intrusive Thoughts Quiet-Mind Aegis

I made this one on a night when my brain felt like a radio between stations. I grabbed a chamomile bag, breathed into the steam, and pictured the thoughts dissolving like sugar in hot water. Three sips later, the static softened. I could hear myself again.

WHEN TO PERFORM THIS SPELL:

Sunday night or during a waning moon

TIME TO ALLOT FOR THE SPELL:

3 minutes

WHERE TO PERFORM THIS SPELL:

Kitchen

INGREDIENTS/TOOLS:

- ◊ Mug
- ◊ 1 chamomile tea bag
- ◊ Hot water
- ◊ Pinch of table salt
- ◊ 1 teaspoon honey

Optional:

Add a pinch of lemon zest.

Directions

1. Set your mug down and say, "Quiet as calm water."
2. Place the tea bag in the mug and pour hot water.
3. Add honey and a tiny pinch of salt.
4. Hold the mug with both hands, breathe in for 4, out for 6, three times.
5. Stir clockwise 3 times and whisper, "Only the thoughts I choose find me."
6. Sip slowly and imagine a gentle hush spreading through your mind.

When shame tried to shrink me, I made a sweet milk blend and spoke to myself like a friend would. The warmth wrapped around my chest. I wasn't perfect, but I was held.

WHEN TO PERFORM THIS SPELL:

Monday morning or any time after a tough co

TIME TO ALLOT FOR THE SPELL:

3 minutes

WHERE TO PERFORM THIS SPELL:

Kitchen

INGREDIENTS/TOOLS:

◊ Small bowl or mug

◊ Warm water

◊ Splash of milk or oat milk

◊ 1 teaspoon honey

◊ Pinch of ground cinnamon

Optional:

Add a drop of vanilla extract.

Directions

1. Combine warm water and a splash of milk.
2. Stir in honey and cinnamon.
3. Cup the bowl and say, "I am worthy of kindness."
4. Take three slow breaths over the steam, imagining a soft cloak around you.
5. Sip and picture the cloak sealing.
6. When you finish, press a hand to your heart and say, "I forgive the human in me."

Old Grudge Release Cut

I carried an old grudge like a stone in my pocket. This lemon ritual gave me a way to cut the sourness and salt it for release. My shoulders finally dropped.

WHEN TO PERFORM THIS SPELL:

Saturday during a waning moon

TIME TO ALLOT FOR THE SPELL:

3 minutes

WHERE TO PERFORM THIS SPELL:

Kitchen

INGREDIENTS/TOOLS:

- ◊ 1 lemon
- ◊ Kitchen knife
- ◊ Small bowl
- ◊ Pinch of salt
- ◊ Water

 Optional:

Add a bay leaf to the bowl.

Directions

1. Fill the bowl with water and add a pinch of salt.
2. Hold the lemon and name the grudge quietly.
3. Slice the lemon in half, saying, "I cut the tie, I keep my peace."
4. Squeeze a bit of juice into the salted water.
5. Drop both halves into the bowl and breathe out as if exhaling the story.
6. Discard the water down the sink and rinse the bowl, visualizing the release.

No Closure Seal Within

Waiting for an apology kept me stuck. Sealing my own jar felt like locking my peace back into place. The quiet came from inside.

WHEN TO PERFORM THIS SPELL:

New moon or any evening you feel

TIME TO ALLOT FOR THE SPELL:

3 minutes

WHERE TO PERFORM THIS SPELL:

Kitchen table

INGREDIENTS/TOOLS:

- ◊ Small jar with lid
- ◊ 1 tablespoon sugar
- ◊ Warm water
- ◊ Small piece of paper
- ◊ Pen

Optional:

Add a pinch of cocoa powder.

Directions

1. On the paper, write: "I seal peace within me."
2. Place sugar in the jar, then the paper on top.
3. Pour in warm water halfway and swirl gently.
4. Say, "What I needed is now given by me."
5. Close the lid firmly. Tap the lid three times.
6. Keep the jar on a shelf for 7 days, then pour it out and recycle the paper.

Self-Blame Forgiveness Charm

After a mistake, I used to replay it on loop. This sweet, spiced sip helped me rewrite the loop with mercy. My chest softened enough to move forward.

WHEN TO PERFORM THIS SPELL:

Any evening, especially after a misstep

TIME TO ALLOT FOR THE SPELL:

3 minutes

WHERE TO PERFORM THIS SPELL:

Kitchen

INGREDIENTS/TOOLS:

- ◊ Mug
- ◊ Warm milk or oat milk
- ◊ 1 teaspoon honey
- ◊ Drop of vanilla extract
- ◊ Pinch of ground cinnamon

Optional:

Add a pinch of nutmeg.

Directions

1. Warm the milk, then add honey and vanilla.
2. Sprinkle cinnamon and watch it bloom on top.
3. Whisper, "I learn, I release, I am still good."
4. Stir clockwise and picture the lesson sinking in.
5. Sip slowly and imagine the blame dissolving.
6. When finished, smile slightly to seal the charm.

Catastrophizing Grounded-Now Anchor

When worst-case storms hit, I cool my hands in iced salt water. It brings me back to now. The panic has less room to spin.

WHEN TO PERFORM THIS SPELL:

Anytime the spiral starts

TIME TO ALLOT FOR THE SPELL:

3 minutes

WHERE TO PERFORM THIS SPELL:

Kitchen sink or counter

INGREDIENTS/TOOLS:

⋄ Medium bowl

⋄ Cold water

⋄ 1 or 2 ice cubes

⋄ Pinch of table salt

⋄ Clean towel or paper towel

Optional:

Add a squeeze of lemon.

Directions

1. Fill the bowl with cold water, add ice and salt.
2. Say, "I anchor in this moment."
3. Submerge your hands up to the wrists for 10 to 20 seconds.
4. Breathe in for 4, out for 6 while focusing on the cool sensation.
5. Dry your hands slowly, noticing the texture.
6. Touch the counter with your palm and name five things you can sense right now.

Perfectionism Freeze Done-is-Good Spell

Perfection used to make me stall. This quick note-and-sip resets me into action mode. Done feels like freedom.

WHEN TO PERFORM THIS SPELL:

Weekday mornings or before starting a task

TIME TO ALLOT FOR THE SPELL:

3 minutes

WHERE TO PERFORM THIS SPELL:

Kitchen table

INGREDIENTS/TOOLS:

◊ Small piece of paper

◊ Pen

◊ Mug

◊ Hot coffee or tea

◊ Pinch of ground cinnamon

Optional:

Add a dash of cocoa powder.

Directions

1. On the paper, write one tiny step you will do next.
2. Place the paper under the mug.
3. Sprinkle cinnamon into your drink and say, "Done is good."
4. Take three sips, feeling energy arrive.
5. Tap the mug gently three times to activate.
6. Do the tiny step immediately.

Boundary Guilt Kind-Guard Affirmation

Saying no used to sting. A peppermint cup and a simple line helped me stand firm without being hard. My yes means more now.

WHEN TO PERFORM THIS SPELL:

Thursday evening or after setting a boundary

TIME TO ALLOT FOR THE SPELL:

3 minutes

WHERE TO PERFORM THIS SPELL:

Kitchen

INGREDIENTS/TOOLS:

◇ Mug

◇ Peppermint tea bag

◇ Hot water

◇ 1 teaspoon honey

◇ Pinch of salt

Optional:

Add a few fresh mint leaves.

Directions

1. Steep peppermint in hot water.
2. Add honey and a tiny pinch of salt for steadiness.
3. Hold the mug and say, "My no protects my yes."
4. Sip and imagine a kind shield forming around you.
5. Repeat the line once more.
6. Finish the cup and keep the line in your pocket for the day.

Fear of Trusting Open-Heart Ward

I wanted to trust again but felt locked. This apple–cinnamon swirl reminded me that hearts can open gradually. Warmth replaced the armor.

WHEN TO PERFORM THIS SPELL:

Friday at sunset or during a waxing moon

TIME TO ALLOT FOR THE SPELL:

3 minutes

WHERE TO PERFORM THIS SPELL:

Kitchen

INGREDIENTS/TOOLS:

- ◊ Small jar with lid
- ◊ Warm water
- ◊ Thin slice of apple
- ◊ Pinch of ground cinnamon
- ◊ 1 teaspoon honey

Optional:

Add a few rose tea leaves.

Directions

1. Place the apple slice in the jar, then add honey and cinnamon.
2. Pour in warm water and close the lid.
3. Swirl gently and say, "I open with wisdom, not fear."
4. Hold the jar at your heart for two breaths.
5. Sip and picture your chest softening like a door unclicking.
6. Thank yourself for courage, even if it is small.

Rest Guilt Permission Rite

Rest used to feel like cheating. This sleepy cup turned permission into a practice. I wake up kinder when I let myself pause.

WHEN TO PERFORM THIS SPELL:

Sunday night or any bedtime

TIME TO ALLOT FOR THE SPELL:

3 minutes

WHERE TO PERFORM THIS SPELL:

Kitchen

INGREDIENTS/TOOLS:

- ◇ Mug
- ◇ Chamomile tea bag
- ◇ Hot water
- ◇ Splash of milk or oat milk
- ◇ Pinch of nutmeg

Optional:

Add a drizzle of honey.

Directions

1. Steep chamomile in hot water.
2. Add a splash of milk and a tiny pinch of nutmeg.
3. Hold the mug and say, "I have permission to rest."
4. Take three slow sips, letting your shoulders drop.
5. Visualize tomorrow you thanking today you.
6. Finish the cup and go to bed without checking your phone.

Chapter 8: Flowing Cycles & Harmony

"Honor the ebb; enjoy the flow."

Your body is rhythmic, not robotic. These quick kitchen spells help you move with your cycle instead of pushing against it. Use them as comfort and confidence rituals alongside any care from your doctor or preferred therapies.

For years I ignored my cycle and then blamed myself for not being a robot. I started Moon Nest Rest by making the bed softer on the days I knew would hurt. Fresh sheets. Heating pad. Tall glass of water. I added Warm Wave Ease. I pressed a warm cloth to my belly and breathed in waves. The first time, I cried because the pain felt seen. I also began a simple calendar note with one word for each day. Fog. Sparks. Lake. Fire. Patterns showed up. I stopped booking hard tasks on Lake days. I put runs on Fire days. I felt like I had a map to my own weather.

One history example. People honored Artemis as a moon guide. The idea is not about perfection. It is about noticing rhythms and giving them space.

This chapter matters because your body has seasons. When you respect them, life feels less like a fight and more like a dance. If you want cooperation instead of shame, let's get started.

Cramps – Warm-Wave Ease

For soothing cycle discomfort.

I built this little ritual on a night when my belly felt like a clenched fist. I warmed a ginger tea, cupped the steam to my skin, and breathed until the tightness loosened. The heat felt like a tide rolling in, then out. My body remembered how to soften.

WHEN TO PERFORM THIS SPELL:

Day 1–3 of your period, evening, or during a v

TIME TO ALLOT FOR THE SPELL:

3 minutes

WHERE TO PERFORM THE SPELL:

Kitchen

INGREDIENTS/TOOLS:

- ◊ Ginger tea bag
- ◊ Honey
- ◊ Ground cinnamon
- ◊ White tealight candle
- ◊ Olive oil

Optional,: To take this spell to the next level, add lavender buds. Not required, but adds an extra layer of energy.

Directions

1. Rub a drop of olive oil on the candle and whisper, "Warm me. Ease me." Light it safely.

2. Steep the ginger tea. Stir in honey and a pinch of cinnamon clockwise for comfort.

3. Hold the mug near your lower belly for a few breaths, then sip slowly and say, "Like water over stone, I soften."

Mood Swings – Balance Spell

For emotional ups and downs.

I tried this on a rollercoaster day. Chamomile, lemon, and sugar felt like three friends pulling me back to center. By the last sip, my edges weren't so sharp.

WHEN TO PERFORM THIS SPELL:

Anytime moods seesaw, morning or sunset

TIME TO ALLOT FOR THE SPELL:

3 minutes

WHERE TO PERFORM THE SPELL:

Kitchen

INGREDIENTS/TOOLS:

- ◊ Chamomile tea bag
- ◊ Lemon slice
- ◊ Sugar
- ◊ White tealight candle
- ◊ Vanilla extract

 Optional,: To take this spell to the next level, add a few rose petals. Not required, but adds an extra layer of energy.

Directions

1. Light the candle and picture a steady, gentle glow around you.
2. Steep chamomile. Add a squeeze of lemon, a pinch of sugar, and a drop of vanilla.
3. Stir once clockwise, once counterclockwise and say, "I allow feelings to move, not rule." Sip.

Bloat & Body Heaviness – Light Comfort

For physical relief and body kindness.

I made this the night my jeans felt like a bad decision. Peppermint, lemon, and a pinch of salt turned heaviness into a light, floaty feeling. I stopped fighting my body and started listening to it.

WHEN TO PERFORM THIS SPELL:

Luteal phase or any time you feel puffy

TIME TO ALLOT FOR THE SPELL:

3 minutes

WHERE TO PERFORM THE SPELL:

Kitchen

INGREDIENTS/TOOLS:

◊ Peppermint tea bag

◊ Lemon slice

◊ Pinch of salt

◊ Cucumber slices

◊ White tealight candle

Optional,: To take this spell to the next level, add fresh mint leaves. Not required, but adds an extra layer of energy.

Directions

1. Light the candle and breathe out heaviness.

2. Steep peppermint. Add lemon, a tiny pinch of salt, and float 1–2 cucumber slices.

3. As you sip, trace a small circle over your belly and say, "I release what I do not need."

Fatigue – Gentle Rally Charm

For low energy days.

This became my kind spark on sluggish mornings. Black tea, honey, orange, and cinnamon gave me a warm nudge instead of a jolt. I didn't power through; I rose up.

WHEN TO PERFORM THIS SPELL:

Morning or mid-afternoon dip

TIME TO ALLOT FOR THE SPELL:

3 minutes

WHERE TO PERFORM THE SPELL:

Kitchen

INGREDIENTS/TOOLS:

◊ Black tea bag

◊ Honey

◊ Orange slice

◊ Ground cinnamon

◊ White tealight candle

 Optional,: To take this spell to the next level, add grated fresh ginger. Not required, but adds an extra layer of energy.

Directions

1. Light the candle and picture a small sun in your chest.
2. Steep black tea. Add honey, a squeeze of orange, and a pinch of cinnamon.
3. Tap the mug lightly and say, "Spark, rise, sustain." Sip with slow, steady breaths.

Irritability – Cool-Edge Calm

For snapping tempers and short patience.

One sharp word too many led me to this. Peppermint sweetness cooled my fuse, while a bay leaf on the counter reminded me to pause. Peace felt like cold water on a hot day.

WHEN TO PERFORM THIS SPELL:

Anytime you feel snappy, especially late aftern

TIME TO ALLOT FOR THE SPELL:

3 minutes

WHERE TO PERFORM THE SPELL:

Kitchen

INGREDIENTS/TOOLS:

◊ Peppermint tea bag

◊ Honey

◊ Bay leaf

◊ Pinch of salt

◊ White tealight candle

Optional,: To take this spell to the next level, add a few chamomile blossoms. Not required, but adds an extra layer of energy.

Directions

1. Place the bay leaf by the candle. Light the candle and breathe out through pursed lips.

2. Steep peppermint. Stir in honey and a tiny pinch of salt to ground.

3. Hold the cup to your heart and say, "Cool head, warm heart." Sip slowly.

Sleep Trouble – Moon-Nest Rest

For luteal phase or restless nights.

This is the night-sip that finally helped me drift. Chamomile with a hint of vanilla and nutmeg turned my thoughts from neon signs into fireflies. My bed felt like a nest again.

WHEN TO PERFORM THIS SPELL:

One hour before bed, anytime you feel wired-

TIME TO ALLOT FOR THE SPELL:

3 minutes

WHERE TO PERFORM THE SPELL:

Kitchen

INGREDIENTS/TOOLS:

◇ Chamomile tea bag

◇ Honey

◇ Ground nutmeg

◇ Vanilla extract

◇ White tealight candle

Optional,: To take this spell to the next level, add a cinnamon stick. Not required, but adds an extra layer of energy.

Directions

1. Dim lights, light the candle, and speak softly: "Night gathers me."

2. Steep chamomile. Add honey, a tiny grate of nutmeg, and a drop of vanilla.

3. Sip in bed or at the table, counting 4 breaths in, 6 out.

Low Desire – Ember Rekindle

For reconnecting to inner spark.

On a day I felt flat, I made spiced cocoa. The heat and sweetness woke up a quiet pulse in me. Not pressure, just permission to feel alive.

WHEN TO PERFORM THIS SPELL:

Date night, self-date night, or anytime your s

TIME TO ALLOT FOR THE SPELL:

3 minutes

WHERE TO PERFORM THE SPELL:

Kitchen

INGREDIENTS/TOOLS:

◊ Cocoa powder

◊ Honey

◊ Ground cinnamon

◊ Cayenne pepper

◊ Red birthday candle

 Optional,: To take this spell to the next level, add a splash of vanilla. Not required, but adds an extra layer of energy.

Directions

1. Dress the red candle with a fingertip of honey, then light it.
2. In hot milk or water, whisk cocoa, honey, a pinch of cinnamon, and the tiniest pinch of cayenne.
3. With the first sip, say, "From ember to glow." Notice warmth spreading.

Cycle Awareness – Rhythm Reminder

For staying connected to your flow.

I kept missing my body's cues until I made this toast ritual. Simple, sweet-spiced, and mindful. It became a daily check-in that made tracking feel kind.

WHEN TO PERFORM THIS SPELL:

Morning during your cycle, especially follicula

TIME TO ALLOT FOR THE SPELL:

3 minutes

WHERE TO PERFORM THE SPELL:

Kitchen

INGREDIENTS/TOOLS:

◇ Slice of bread

◇ Butter

◇ Ground cinnamon

◇ Sugar

◇ White tealight candle

Optional,: To take this spell to the next level, add a drizzle of honey. Not required, but adds an extra layer of energy.

Directions

1. Light the candle and take one honest breath: "How do I feel today?"

2. Toast bread. Butter it. Sprinkle cinnamon and sugar.

3. Before the first bite, trace a small circle on the toast and say, "I move with my rhythm." Eat slowly.

Stigma Stress – Quiet-Pride Shield

For shame or secrecy around your period.

A heavy comment once left me small. This little kitchen ward helped me stand upright again. Salt, oil, rosemary, lemon. Simple protection. Quiet pride.

WHEN TO PERFORM THIS SPELL:

Before school, work, or social events; on the fi

TIME TO ALLOT FOR THE SPELL:

3 minutes

WHERE TO PERFORM THE SPELL:

Kitchen

INGREDIENTS/TOOLS:

- ◊ Coarse salt
- ◊ Olive oil
- ◊ Dried rosemary
- ◊ Lemon peel
- ◊ White tealight candle

Optional,: To take this spell to the next level, add a bay leaf. Not required, but adds an extra layer of energy.

Directions

1. Light the candle. In a small dish, mix a pinch of salt, a drop of oil, and a pinch of rosemary.

2. Rub the mixture lightly over your hands, then rinse. Swipe lemon peel over your wrists.

3. Say, "I am natural. I am safe. I am seen." Step out with steady shoulders.

Doctor Visit Nerves – Advocacy Voice Charm

For appointments where you need to speak up.

I made this before a visit I was dreading. A bold tea and a pocket mint reminded me I had a voice. I walked in calm and clear.

WHEN TO PERFORM THIS SPELL:

The morning of your appointment or while ge

TIME TO ALLOT FOR THE SPELL:

3 minutes

WHERE TO PERFORM THE SPELL:

Kitchen

INGREDIENTS/TOOLS:

- ◊ Black tea bag
- ◊ Honey
- ◊ Lemon slice
- ◊ Peppermint candy
- ◊ Bay leaf

 Optional,: To take this spell to the next level, add a sprig of basil. Not required, but adds an extra layer of energy.

Directions

1. Steep black tea. Add honey and lemon.
2. Hold the bay leaf and breathe, saying, "My voice is steady and heard." Tuck it into your pocket.
3. Keep the peppermint candy for the waiting room. Let it melt as you repeat, "I can ask. I can advocate."

These rituals are supportive practices and not a substitute for medical care. Always listen to your body and consult a healthcare professional when needed.

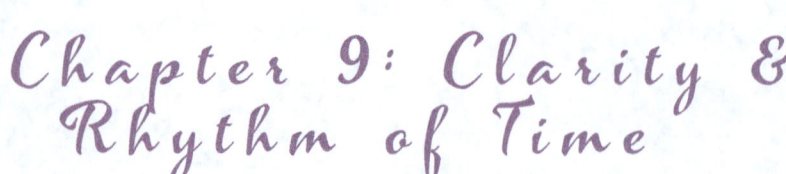

Chapter 9: Clarity & Rhythm of Time

"When you can't find time, make rhythm."

You are not late. You are out of sync. This chapter is your gentle metronome, helping you line up action with intention so your day stops fighting you. Each spell is fast, kitchen-friendly, and built to turn vague overwhelm into bite-sized moves you can actually do.

I used to end every day sure I had failed. I built a small Results Meter with three wooden beads on a string. Each night I slid one bead for one thing that moved. Washed the dishes. Sent the email. Read two pages. After a week, the beads looked like a soft ladder. I felt proof I could climb. On hard mornings I used Two Minute Spark. I set a timer and cleaned my desk for two minutes. Often the timer rang and I kept going. If not, at least I had a clear surface. That made the next step easier.

One history example. Monasteries used bells to divide the day into focused blocks. Work. Prayer. Rest. The bell was a kind boss that helped people switch tasks.

This chapter matters because time feels scary when it is just a blur. Simple rhythms give your day bones and breath. If you want progress you can see and a week that resets on purpose, let's get started.

Overwhelm: Sorting it Out Spell

For sorting what truly matters.

I tried this on a day my to-do list felt like a junk drawer. I watched spices behave in water and suddenly saw it: some things dissolve quickly when I tend to them, some sink and can wait, some float on top like noise. The glass became a tiny map. My head unclenched.

WHEN TO PERFORM THIS SPELL:

Morning, or any time you feel swamped

TIME TO ALLOT FOR THE SPELL:

3 minutes

WHERE TO PERFORM THE SPELL:

Kitchen counter

INGREDIENTS/TOOLS:

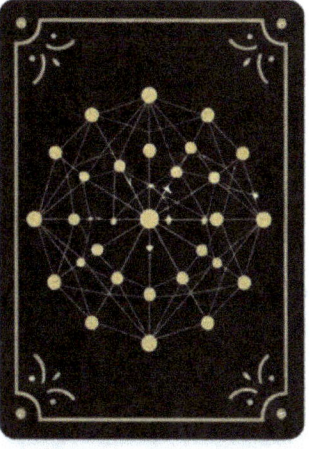

- ◇ Clear glass
- ◇ 1 cup water
- ◇ Pinch of salt
- ◇ Pinch of ground cinnamon
- ◇ 7 grains of dry rice

 Optional: Add a bay leaf. Not required, but adds an extra layer of focus.

Directions

1. Fill the glass with water. Breathe in for 4, out for 4.

2. Whisper, "Show me what actually matters."

3. Sprinkle salt and say, "Now tasks." Tap cinnamon on top and say, "Later tasks." Drop the rice and say, "Schedule tasks."

4. Watch: salt vanishes first, rice sinks slow, cinnamon floats. Let that image sort your list into Now, Schedule, Later.

5. Say, "I act in the right order," then pour the water down the sink to release the noise.

Stuck Slump: Block-Buster Thaw

For breaking stagnant energy.

One gray afternoon, my mood felt frozen. I salted ice, lit a tiny light, and listened to the gentle crackle as the cubes softened. The air shifted. So did I.

WHEN TO PERFORM THIS SPELL:

Any afternoon you feel stuck

TIME TO ALLOT FOR THE SPELL:

3 minutes

WHERE TO PERFORM THE SPELL:

By the kitchen sink

INGREDIENTS/TOOLS:

◊ Small bowl

◊ 3 ice cubes

◊ Lemon wedge

◊ Pinch of salt

◊ White tealight candle

Optional: Add a pinch of rosemary. Not required, but adds an extra layer of clearing.

Directions

1. Place ice in the bowl. Sprinkle salt.

2. Squeeze the lemon over the cubes.

3. Light the tealight beside the bowl. Say, "Block, thaw. Mood, flow."

4. Watch the first wet sheen appear. Imagine your slump melting with it.

5. Snuff the candle safely. Pour the bowl into the sink and rinse the bowl clean.

Time Blindness: Tuner Rite

For better awareness of passing time.

I used to look up and wonder where an hour went. This tea taught me what three minutes feels like in my bones. Now my body keeps a quiet beat.

WHEN TO PERFORM THIS SPELL:

Morning, before tasks

TIME TO ALLOT FOR THE SPELL:

3 minutes

WHERE TO PERFORM THE SPELL:

Kitchen

INGREDIENTS/TOOLS:

- ◊ Mug
- ◊ Any tea bag
- ◊ Hot water
- ◊ Spoon
- ◊ Pinch of sugar

Optional: Add a slice of lemon. Not required, but adds a bright focus.

Directions

1. Add tea to the mug and pour hot water.
2. Close your eyes. Breathe slow and count 12 steady breaths.
3. When you reach 12, stir clockwise 3 times with the spoon. This is your 3-minute felt sense.
4. Add a pinch of sugar and say, "I can feel time passing."
5. Sip once, then start your first task while that inner beat is fresh.

Fear of Mistakes: Safe Starter

For beginning without pressure to be perfect.

My first drafts used to terrify me. Three wax drops on a salted plate taught me to love ugly starts. Progress appeared the moment I let it.

WHEN TO PERFORM THIS SPELL:

Right before starting a new task

TIME TO ALLOT FOR THE SPELL:

3 minutes

WHERE TO PERFORM THE SPELL:

Kitchen table

INGREDIENTS/TOOLS:

- ◊ White candle
- ◊ Lighter or matches
- ◊ Small plate
- ◊ 1 teaspoon olive oil
- ◊ Pinch of salt

Optional: Add a clove. Not required, but adds a protective push.

Directions

1. Rub a thin smear of oil on the plate, then sprinkle salt in a small circle.
2. Light the candle. Hold it over the center and let 3 drops of wax fall.
3. Say, "First is for showing up. Second is for learning. Third is for momentum."
4. Snuff the candle. Touch the cooled wax and whisper, "Done beats perfect."
5. Start your task immediately with a tiny first step.

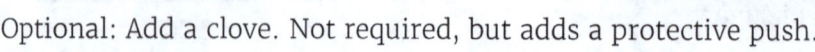

Decision Paralysis: Yes-Meter Discernment

For choosing between too many options.

My head spins when choices multiply. Two fizzing glasses gave me a simple test and a body yes I could trust.

WHEN TO PERFORM THIS SPELL:

When comparing two options

TIME TO ALLOT FOR THE SPELL:

3 minutes

WHERE TO PERFORM THE SPELL:

Kitchen counter

INGREDIENTS/TOOLS:

- ◇ 2 small glasses
- ◇ White vinegar
- ◇ Baking soda
- ◇ Teaspoon
- ◇ Paper towel

Optional: Add a basil leaf. Not required, but adds clarity.

Directions

1. Pour equal vinegar into both glasses.
2. Point to Glass A and speak Option A aloud. Drop the same small spoonful of baking soda in. Watch and feel.
3. Point to Glass B, speak Option B, repeat the same spoonful. Watch and feel.
4. Notice which fizz made your chest feel open or your breath ease. That is your yes.
5. Say, "I choose and move," then wipe the counter and pour both glasses down the sink.

Routine Won't Stick: Habit Hook

For creating steady rhythms.

I kept forgetting my tiny habits. A jar with beans turned invisible goals into a rhythm I could see and touch.

WHEN TO PERFORM THIS SPELL:

Sunday evening, or the night before a new rou

TIME TO ALLOT FOR THE SPELL:

3 minutes

WHERE TO PERFORM THE SPELL:

Kitchen shelf

INGREDIENTS/TOOLS:

◇ Small jar

◇ Handful of dried beans or pasta shells

◇ Bay leaf

◇ Pinch of salt

◇ Rubber band

Optional: Add a sprig of thyme. Not required, but adds staying power.

Directions

1. Put the beans into the jar. Slip the rubber band around the jar's middle.

2. Slip the bay leaf inside against the glass, sprinkle a pinch of salt over the beans.

3. Hold the jar and say, "One action, repeated, becomes rhythm."

4. Place the jar where you will see it daily. Each day you complete the habit, slide the rubber band up a bit. If you miss, slide it down.

5. At week's end, empty the beans, reset, and repeat.

Too Many Goals: Power Cut

For trimming to what's essential.

I wanted to chase everything. A little oil on a plate showed me the three grains that truly belonged this week.

WHEN TO PERFORM THIS SPELL:

Monday morning or new moon

TIME TO ALLOT FOR THE SPELL:

3 minutes

WHERE TO PERFORM THE SPELL:

Kitchen table

INGREDIENTS/TOOLS:

◇ Plate

◇ 1 teaspoon olive oil

◇ Pinch of dry rice

◇ Pinch of black pepper

◇ White candle

 Optional: Add a pinch of ground ginger. Not required, but adds decisive fire.

Directions

1. Rub a coin-sized circle of oil in the center of the plate.

2. Name each goal and drop one grain of rice onto the center for it.

3. Sprinkle pepper around the outer edge to represent distractions.

4. Light the candle and gently blow across the plate. Grains that stick in the oil are your essentials. The rest can wait.

5. Say, "I cut power to the extra," then snuff the candle.

Starting Trouble: Two-Minute Spark

For moving past resistance.

On sleepy mornings, I make a tiny cup that tastes like courage. Two sips later, I'm already moving.

WHEN TO PERFORM THIS SPELL:

Right before the first task of the day

TIME TO ALLOT FOR THE SPELL:

3 minutes

WHERE TO PERFORM THE SPELL:

Kitchen

INGREDIENTS/TOOLS:

- ◊ Mug
- ◊ 1 teaspoon instant coffee or cocoa
- ◊ Hot water
- ◊ Pinch of ground cinnamon
- ◊ Spoon

 Optional: Add a drop of vanilla extract. Not required, but adds warm motivation.

Directions

1. Add coffee or cocoa to the mug. Pour hot water halfway.
2. Stir in a pinch of cinnamon and say, "Spark on. Start small."
3. Take two mindful sips. Feel warmth wake your chest and hands.
4. Put the spoon down, stand up, and take one tiny action within 60 seconds.
5. Keep the mug nearby as your anchor until the first action is done.

Creative Block: Muse Tap Knock

For inviting inspiration back.

When my ideas hide, I call them with sound and scent. A wooden knock and vanilla trail brings the muse back like a friend.

WHEN TO PERFORM THIS SPELL:

Evening, or any time your mind feels flat

TIME TO ALLOT FOR THE SPELL:

3 minutes

WHERE TO PERFORM THE SPELL:

Kitchen table or counter

INGREDIENTS/TOOLS:

- ◇ Wooden spoon
- ◇ Cutting board
- ◇ Vanilla extract
- ◇ Glass of water
- ◇ Tealight candle

 Optional: Add a pinch of nutmeg. Not required, but adds imaginative lift.

Directions

1. Dab a tiny bit of vanilla on your wrists.
2. Knock the wooden spoon on the cutting board 3 times in a steady rhythm.
3. Light the candle and say, "Muse, I am listening."
4. Sip water, close your eyes, and notice the first image, word, or feeling that arrives.
5. Capture it immediately in your notes app or on a scrap, then start.

Weekly Reset: Recast Wheel

For closing a week and starting fresh.

By Friday I used to feel scattered. Rolling a lemon like a small sun helped me end the week clean and start the next with aim.

WHEN TO PERFORM THIS SPELL:

Friday night or Sunday afternoon

TIME TO ALLOT FOR THE SPELL:

3 minutes

WHERE TO PERFORM THE SPELL:

Kitchen table

INGREDIENTS/TOOLS:

- ◊ Lemon or orange
- ◊ Plate
- ◊ 1 teaspoon olive oil
- ◊ Pinch of salt
- ◊ White candle

Optional: Add a sprig of lavender. Not required, but adds calm closure.

Directions

1. Place the citrus on the plate. Light the candle.
2. Roll the fruit clockwise while saying 3 wins from the week.
3. Roll it counterclockwise while naming 3 lessons you are releasing.
4. Rub a little oil on the fruit, sprinkle with a pinch of salt, and say, "Wheel turns. I start fresh."
5. Snuff the candle. Use the citrus in tomorrow's meal as a bright reset.

These are not chores. They are tiny rituals that bring rhythm back to your minutes. When your day plays to a beat, you stop tripping and start dancing.

Your Power, Your Path

You began this journey wondering if magick was too complicated or only meant for someone else. Along the way, you discovered that it is already yours. You saw how a pinch of salt can clear your voice when texts feel impossible, how a simple leaf can steady you before walking into a new room, and how one circle on a page can protect your focus when your mind is spinning. These were never just spells. They were reminders of what was already inside you.

This book is not something you read once and set aside. It is a companion you can return to whenever life feels loud, whenever you need grounding, protection, confidence, or love. Each time you open these pages, something new may speak to you, because magick grows as you grow. The tools are simple, but the power is you.

If these spells have helped you, I would love to hear your story. You can find a QR code that takes you straight to leave a review. It means more than you know, because your words may be the spark that helps another reader begin.It only takes a minute. And if you felt this book was a gift in your own life, consider sharing a copy with someone you care about. It is one of the most unforgettable gifts you can give: the reminder that they already hold magick within them.

So whenever you need it, return here. Let these spells meet you again, in every new chapter of your life. And never forget the truth that runs through every page: you are the spell.

Direct Review Link:

Would you leave a quick review?

Even one sentence makes a huge difference and takes just a minute.

As a small author, your feedback really matters & lifts my hearth.

Thank you for being part of this journey!

Other books you might find interesting:

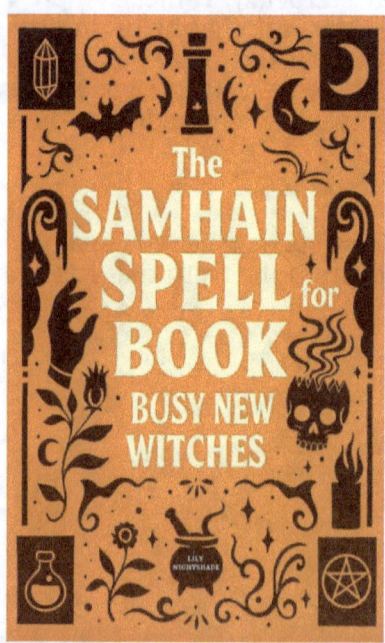

www.ingramcontent.com/pod-product-compliance
Lightning Source LLC
Chambersburg PA
CBHW071522120626
46550CB00006B/2318